Battles of the Uga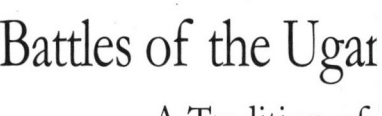
A Tradition of

Muhoozi Kainerugaba

FOUNTAIN PUBLISHERS
Kampala

Fountain Publishers
P. O. Box 488
Kampala - Uganda
E-mail: sales@fountainpublishers.co.ug
publishing@fountainpublishers.co.ug
Website: www.fountainpublishers.co.ug

Distributed in Europe and Commonwealth countries outside Africa by:
African Books Collective, P.O. Box 721, Oxford OX1 9EN, UK.
Tel: 44(0) 1869 349110, Fax:+44(0)1869 349110
E-mail: orders@africanbookscollective.com
Website: www.africanbookscollective.com

Distributed in North America by:
Michigan State University Press
1405 South Harrison Road
25 Manly Miles Building
East Lansing, MI 48823-5245
Tel: +1 517 3559543, 800 6782120
Fax: +1 517 4322611
E-mail: msupress@.msu.edu
Website: www.msupress.msu.edu

© Muhoozi Kainerugaba 2010
First published 2010

All rights reserved. No part of this publication may be reprinted or reproduced or utilised in any form or by any means, electronic, mechanical or other means now known or hereafter invented, including copying and recording, or in any information storage or retrieval system, without permission in writing from the publishers.

ISBN 978-9970-25-032-5

Cover photo: Heroes of the Resistance War:
Gen. Salim Saleh and Fred Rwigema

Contents

List of Abbreviations and Acronyms... *viii*
Preface .... *xi*

Chapter 1	Is there an African Way of War?..	1
Chapter 2	Mbale 1973: 'Cometh the Hour, Cometh the Man'..	17
Chapter 3	To Start a War..	47

Picture Section A... 56

Chapter 4	The Clarion Call: First Battle of Kabamba...............	61
Chapter 5	Bukalabi: Saleh's Baptism in Fire.................................	78
Chapter 6	Masindi: Mobile Brigade Transforms the War..........	90
Chapter 7	The Third Battle of Kabamba: 'The Beginning of the End'..	110
Chapter 8	Battle of Kembogo: The Enemy's Center of Gravity is Shattered.......................................	125
Chapter 9	The Investment of Masaka...	141
Chapter 10	Kampala	155

Picture Section B... 183

Chapter 11	What Was the Strategy of the Resistance War?.........	191
Chapter 12	The Nexus between Historical Experience and Doctrine..	204
Chapter 13	Epilogue: Maneuver in Our Future	215
Index	....	220

For my father, Yoweri Kaguta Museveni

my mother, Janet Kataha Museveni

my wife, Charlotte

and our children,

Ruhamya, Kenshuro and Ihunde

About the Author

Lt. Colonel Muhoozi Kainerugaba was born in 1974 in Dar es Salaam Tanzania, where his father Yoweri Museveni was conducting an underground campaign to oust Idi Amin. He moved back to Uganda briefly with his mother and sisters in 1979 (with the downfall of the Amin regime) before being forced back into exile in 1981.

He had his early education in Tanzania, Kenya, Sweden and Uganda. In 1994, he joined Nottingham University in the United Kingdom, three years later he graduated with a BA (Hons) degree in Politics. Muhoozi joined the UPDF in 1999 as an officer cadet, that same year he went to attend the commissioning course at the Royal Military Academy Sandhurst in the United Kingdom.

In 2000, he was commissioned as Second Lieutenant in the UPDF. After a number of assignments and courses, in 2003, Muhoozi was promoted to the rank of Major. He was placed in charge of the fledgling Motorized Infantry Battalion within the Presidential Guard Brigade. Later in 2007, he enrolled at the Command and General Staff College at Fort Leavenworth Kansas, USA. He graduated in June of 2008. In July of that year, he became the UPDF's first paratrooper after graduating from the US Army's Airborne School in Fort Benning, Georgia. He was promoted to the rank of Lieutenant Colonel and appointed Commander of Special Forces in the UPDF.

In 2007, he participated in the defeat of the ADF in Bundibugyo. In 2008, he was deployed as the Land Component Commander of Operation Lightning Thunder that has succeeded in weakening the LRA in the DRC and Central African Republic. Muhoozi married Charlotte Kutesa in 1999 and they have been blessed with three children.

List of Abbreviations and Acronyms

AAA	Anti Aircraft Artillery
AAG	Anti Aircraft Gun
AO	Area of Operations
APC	Armored Personnel Carrier
BMATT	British Military Assistance Training Team
BTR 60	Bronetransportyor (Russian Armored Personnel Carrier)
C3	Command, Control, Communications
C4ISR	Command, Control, Communications, Computers, Intelligence, Surveillance, Reconnaissance
CAR	Central African Republic
CDF	Chief of Defense Forces
CHC	Chairman of High Command
CIA	Central Intelligence Agency
COG	Center of Gravity
COP	Common Operating Picture
COT	Chief of Operations and Training
CP	Command Post
CSM	Company Sergeant Major
DRC	Democratic Republic of Congo
DS	Directing Staff
FOO	Forward Observation Officer
FRELIMO	Frente de Libertação de Moçambique/ Front for the Liberation of Mozambique
FRONASA	Front for National Salvation
FTX	Field Training Exercise

FUP	Form Up Place
H-hour	Hour of Attack/Specific Time an Operation or Exercise Begins
IDF	Israeli Defense Force
JO I	Junior Officer Class I
JO II	Junior Officer Class II
KAR	King's African Rifles
LD	Line of Departure
LRA	Lord's Resistance Army
LTC	Lieutenant Colonel
ME	Main Effort
MG	Major General
MHC	Member of High Command
NATO	North Atlantic Treaty Organization
NCO	Non-Commissioned Officer
NRA	National Resistance Army
NRM	National Resistance Movement
OBUA	Operations in Built-Up Areas
OODA	Observation, Orientation, Decision, Action
OPSEC	Operational Security
PGM	Precision Guided Munitions
PLA	People's Liberation Army
PLO	Palestinian Liberation Organization
POW	Prisoner of War
RIF	Reduction in Force
RMA	Revolution in Military Affairs

RV	Rendevouz point
SLR	Self Loading Rifle
SO	Senior Officer
SOPs	Standard Operating Procedures
TAMs	Tactical Aide Memoire
TEWT	Tactical Exercise Without Troops
TLPs	Troop Leading Procedures
TOE	Table of Organization and Equipment
TPDF	Tanzanian People's Defense Forces
TTPs	Tactics, Techniques and Procedures
UNLA	Uganda National Liberation Army
UNLF	Uganda National Liberation Front
UNRF	Uganda National Rescue Front
UPC	Uganda People's Congress
UPDF	Uganda People's Defense Forces
USARF	University Students' African Revolutionary Front
USFS	Uganda Soviet Friendship Society
UVSC	Uganda Vietnam Solidarity Committee
2i/c	Second in Command

Preface

In the fall of 2007, around the month of October, I was preparing a paper on the National Resistance Army/Uganda Peoples' Defense Force's Reduction in Force (RIF) exercise of the early 1990s, for my Force Management class at the Command and General Staff College (Fort Leavenworth). As part of the research for this paper and others (that dealt with the African military scene), I experienced the dearth of information relating to this field. Whatever little information there was, often was written by foreigners who inevitably had superficial or skewed perceptions on these issues. Of course, because of my voracious appetite for literature dealing with the history of the continent, I had noticed this for many years prior to this particular period. I remember searching through the shelves at the library for hours on end for authentic African voices tackling African issues. I was quite concerned that the African viewpoint was not being communicated to those elements abroad who might be interested in the security scene of the continent. Finally, in frustration I managed to procure a few books from back home and donated them to the library.

    The idea of writing a book (which I had always had), gathered momentum. I felt it was an obligation for more Africans to articulate the continent's history and dynamics, something only they could do with some degree of accuracy. However, it was also clear to me that this was only half of the process of helping the continent. It was also incumbent upon those external actors who claim an interest in Africa's progress, to endeavour to understand these African voices. In essence, they have to become dedicated and humble students of Africa. Often, I observed an outward genuflecting to what was perceived as 'African interests', however, one always sensed an underlying haughtiness and condescension that obfuscated the real issues for some of these individuals. The reaction of many Africans to this sort of attitude is simply to disregard it, and continue with whatever course they are set upon. The result is that you have a situation where people are operating on different planes, seemingly interacting, networking without any positive outcomes.

In my opinion this is at the heart of the international community's incessant misreading of Africa and African events. Then in the wake of some African tragedy they ask themselves, 'what did we miss?' This soul searching after the fact only rubs vinegar into the wounds of African societies that have been shattered by war, ethnic strife, economic collapse or genocide. A phrase I continually heard at Leavenworth seems apt, in instances like the genocides in Rwanda and Darfur, the Lord's Resistance Army's (LRA) terrorism in northern Uganda, Democratic Republic of Congo (DRC) and Central African Republic (CAR), the bloody chaos in Somalia, the west can justifiably be accused of 'drinking the Kool Aid'.* In this instance the 'Kool Aid' is the west's own negative (and backward) perceptions of Africa and Africans.

True, Africa's progress is primarily an African matter, it is Africans who will develop the continent (just like they liberated it from colonialism and Apartheid), but for those friends of Africa

---

*   Drinking the kool aid' is an American expression that means accepting an argument or philosophy wholeheartedly, without question. Generally taken to mean blind acceptance of something. It was coined after the Jonestown massacre of 1978, where followers of a cult committed mass suicide at the behest of their leader by drinking Kool Aid laced with cyanide.

(who are genuinely interested in the continent's development) they must be modest; it is impossible for anyone (especially foreigners) to understand this vast and complex continent without humility. Unless both parties really start communicating, the continent's vital interests will continue to be 'lost in translation'.

The Ugandan resistance war is an interesting study in precisely this inexplicable lack of communication between Africa and the West. For decades the West chose to discount the horrors that were being perpetuated against the people of Uganda, first under Milton Obote, then Idi Amin and once more under Obote's second government. Milton Obote's second and infinitely more brutal regime (1981-1985) was actively supported by some western governments. The people of Uganda by their own means fought and overthrew this oppressive system, writing a glorious history for posterity. Symptomatic of the misinterpretations of the continent that often find currency in the west, was that this genuinely nationalist movement was misrepresented as socialist-inclined during the cold war epoch. Yoweri Museveni's immortal words, in the Luwero Triangle, in response to a question posed by a western journalist hit home; the journalist had asked if the Ugandan resistance movement was 'pro-east or pro-west?' 'We are pro-ourselves', the intense rebel leader replied.

This book is principally concerned with the military aspects of the resistance war. I have presented a limited and technical vista of the war, choosing to focus on individual battles. This is for a number of reasons. First of all, I feel some of the existing books on the resistance war deal with the larger issues that led to (and sustained) the conflagration quite well. In this regard, I would recommend *Sowing the Mustard Seed* written by Yoweri Museveni and *Museveni's Long March* by Ondoga ori Amaza. Since the focus of these books is primarily the history of the resistance movement, their handling of the war is panoramic and characterised by broad sweeps.

Secondly, as an active duty military officer in the UPDF, I felt that a more penetrating investigation of the battles of the resistance war would be more beneficial in the narrow sense (as an individual) and more broadly as an institution. Hence, this book is part of my self-education in the conduct and nature of war, something I believe is a necessary and continuous process for all military professionals. As an institution the Uganda Peoples' Defense Forces (UPDF) has achieved feats that are very difficult to describe to those who aren't conversant with our history. The UPDF's predecessor the National Resistance Army (NRA) fought an arduous and autonomous guerrilla war in the center of the country against a determined and tough adversary. As was suggested above, this adversary, the Uganda National Liberation Army, was amply supported by external forces. After the overthrow of the dictatorships in 1986, the NRA/UPDF fought a series of brutal counter-insurgency wars against a host of rebel factions determined to reverse the gains of the people of Uganda. The NRA/UPDF also supported the struggles of the people of Rwanda, Southern Sudan and the DRC. The UPDF is currently the principal force supporting the people of Somalia in their fight against religious extremism. The UPDF has therefore been a transformational force in the history of eastern and central Africa; it has made a contribution to the struggle for freedom of the peoples of this region far beyond anything that preceded it.

As the UPDF continues to expand its capabilities, it is critical that we develop a thorough understanding of the elements in our 'genetics' (as an institution) that made us so successful. This awareness will have an impact on our current efforts to formulate a doctrine that is pertinent to our history and circumstances. It is my hope that this study (which draws its vitality from our historical experience) will contribute to that process. In this regard, the theme of this book is a consideration of what the nature of the war was, i.e. was it characterized by maneuver or by battles of annihilation? Basing upon the answer to this question, inferences are made about the suitable doctrinal philosophy for the UPDF.

My thesis is that the Ugandan resistance war featured some battles of annihilation like the decisive battle of Kembogo but was decidedly a campaign based on maneuver. Guerrilla wars are by their nature predicated on a maneuverist approach to operations, and this held true in the Ugandan experience.

The first chapter attempts to position the Ugandan resistance war in the broader history of warfare in Africa (specifically Ugandan warfare). It is a cursory but important consideration of whether an African theme to warfare exists? The answer to this question should be important for African military professionals because it provides for continuity between the continent's past and future. The native states in Africa prior to the colonial era had developed warfare to a level where some of these states like Ethiopia were able to defeat the aggressions of the colonialists. The 'African way of war' merits further investigation, there are deep and crucial lessons waiting to be discovered by Africa's cerebral soldiers and military historians.

Chapter two contemplates the clandestine phase of the resistance war. This was the time before the commencement of open kinetic operations (1981-1985). There are similarities between revolutionary clandestine operations and conventional special operations that this chapter highlights. Yoweri Museveni once remarked that he was engaged in 'special operations' in the 70s, a statement borne out by the facts that emerge in this chapter. The chapter focuses on the events surrounding the incident at 49 Maluku Estate in Mbale.

The third chapter is the bridge between the first two chapters and the rest of the book. It attempts to assess the psychological elements that make the waging and sustaining of a war (especially a people's war) possible. What is it that can drive men to be willing to throw everything away in the faint hope that change may result? As a soldier this question is especially fascinating. There is a world of difference between being a soldier in a national army fighting insurgencies (which is what I have experienced) and being a combatant in a rebel army fighting to overthrow an established regime. It must be a special mix of factors that combine to produce a fighting force willing to pay the ultimate price for a cause for which there is no guarantee will succeed.

In the subsequent seven chapters, I examine battles that I feel provide some lessons for the present day UPDF. I have endeavoured to select battles (out of the countless battles that were fought throughout the five year struggle) for each phase of the war. According to Maoist theory and practice, there are three phases to a people's war. These are: guerrilla warfare; mobile warfare; and regular/conventional warfare. Therefore, I have endeavoured to select battles for each of these phases starting with guerrilla warfare naturally. Hence, the first battle of Kabamba and the battle of Bukalabi were fought in the guerrilla warfare phase of the struggle. Masindi and the third battle of Kabamba represent the mobile warfare stage of the war and finally Masaka and Kampala symbolize the accession to conventional warfare.

The battle of Kembogo which is also studied in this book (chapter 8) was the definitive engagement that signalled the transition of the war from the mobile warfare phase to the conventional phase. It is also analysized because it was the most decisive battle in the whole resistance war. It represents one of the few battles of annihilation in a war that was largely maneuverist in nature as I indicated above.

Chapter 11 attempts to investigate what the strategy of the resistance war was. It asks the question: What was the strategy of the Ugandan Resistance War? The almost ritualized answer to this for decades now has been that the resistance war adhered to Mao's people's war strategy. This chapter supports that position to a point but veers off this well trodden path to make some interesting findings. This complicated and convoluted subject merits scrutiny. The results in this chapter will, at the minimum, be interesting and hopefully will stimulate more study.

Chapter 12 argues the point that there is a link between our historical experience and any doctrine that we may promulgate today or in the future. During the writing of this book, some of the senior officers I interviewed were at pains to understand the relevance to the present day of events that occurred 24 to 29 years ago. This is a major problem in Africa, where we live in the moment and once that moment passes we do not seek to record it and extract lessons that will serve us well in similar (or dissimilar) situations in the future. Therefore, we are constantly re-inventing the wheel instead of making our wealth of experiences work for us. Otto von Bismarck said, 'Only a fool learns from experience. I learn from the experiences of others', a suitable description of our endless re-learning of past lessons, which should be part of our collective memory and reflexive defenses.

This was one of the reasons why Africa was over-run by colonial invasion in the past, the absence of recorded and stored collective experiences. Additionally, this reluctance to profit from past experiences can only be described as imperceptive, because all 'revolutions in military affairs' have been based on a careful and thorough analysis of past wars. Astute military organizations have always based innovation in war on concrete historical case studies. Therefore, this chapter seeks to show the direct and urgent relevance of the resistance war to our present day attempts at drafting doctrine.

The final chapter is a petition for the adoption of a maneuverist doctrine; this naturally is based on the facts that emerge in the preceding chapters. Maneuver is in our genetic make up as a military institution. It was maneuver that unlocked the gate to victory in the resistance war. We cannot separate ourselves from who we are; the scions of a great maneuverist tradition.

This book would not have been possible without the support of a number of people. I would like to express my profound thanks to the President of the Republic of Uganda and Commander-in-Chief of the Armed Forces, General Yoweri Kaguta Museveni. He offered wise guidance throughout the writing of this book, never once did he hesitate to make time to meet and discuss with me, often in the midst of busy schedules or in his preciously limited free time. I would like to thank all the senior UPDF officers who consented to being interviewed, these include General Elly Tumwine, General Salim Saleh 'Rufu', the late Major General James Kazini, Brigadier Steven Kashaka, Brigadier John Mugume and Colonel Sam Kavuma. I had the good fortune to interview the late Major General James Kazini on two occasions in February 2009 and June 2009 (only five months before his tragic death); he was one of the few senior officers who eagerly embraced and actively encouraged the recording of our great history. He was also a dear friend of mine and I shall miss him very much. Rest in peace afande! The completion of this book is largely due to the tremendous insights that all these men shared with me.

I would also like to thank and recognize Mr. and Mrs. Maumbe Mukwana for their help in making Chapter 3 a reality (the story of the 49 Maluku incident). I sat with each of them separately and the information from these interviews was helpful. I must mention William H. McRaven and Robert Leonhard both American authors whose books *Spec Ops: Case Studies in Special Operations Warfare Theory and Practice* and *The Art of Maneuver* respectively made an impression on me. The chapters dealing with the battles are organized in much the same way as McRaven's case studies in his seminal book. Much of the concepts dealing with maneuver are borrowed from Leonhard's penetrative treatise on maneuver warfare. I must also acknowledge the role played by the writings of Carl von Clausewitz and Mao Zedong in the making of this book. These two men are probably the foremost theorists of war and strategy that history has thus far produced. It is, consequently, nearly impossible to write anything on war without referring to them.

I must thank James Tumusime, Managing Director of Fountain Publishers as well as Mariam Nakisekka, Daniel Twebaze and Robert Sempagala-Mpagi (staff members at Fountain Publishers) for their patience and steadfast work in preparing this book. I am much obliged for your efforts.

Finally, I would like to thank my wife Charlotte and our beautiful children Ruhamya, Kenshuro and Ihunde for their continued love and support. Charlotte, thank you for your keen eye for punctuation marks and for editing parts of this book before it went to the publishers. This book would not have been possible without you all. My heartfelt thanks go out to all of you!

Muhoozi Kainerugaba
Entebbe, Uganda
May 2010

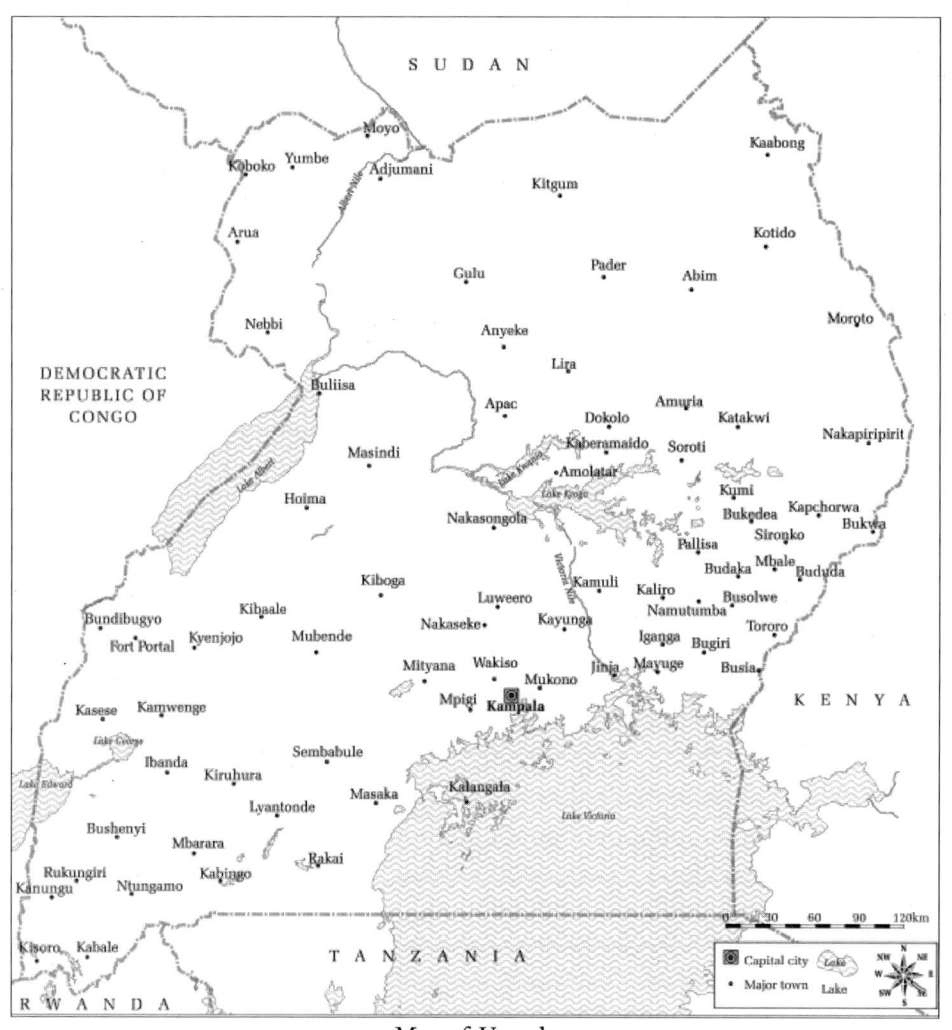

Map of Uganda

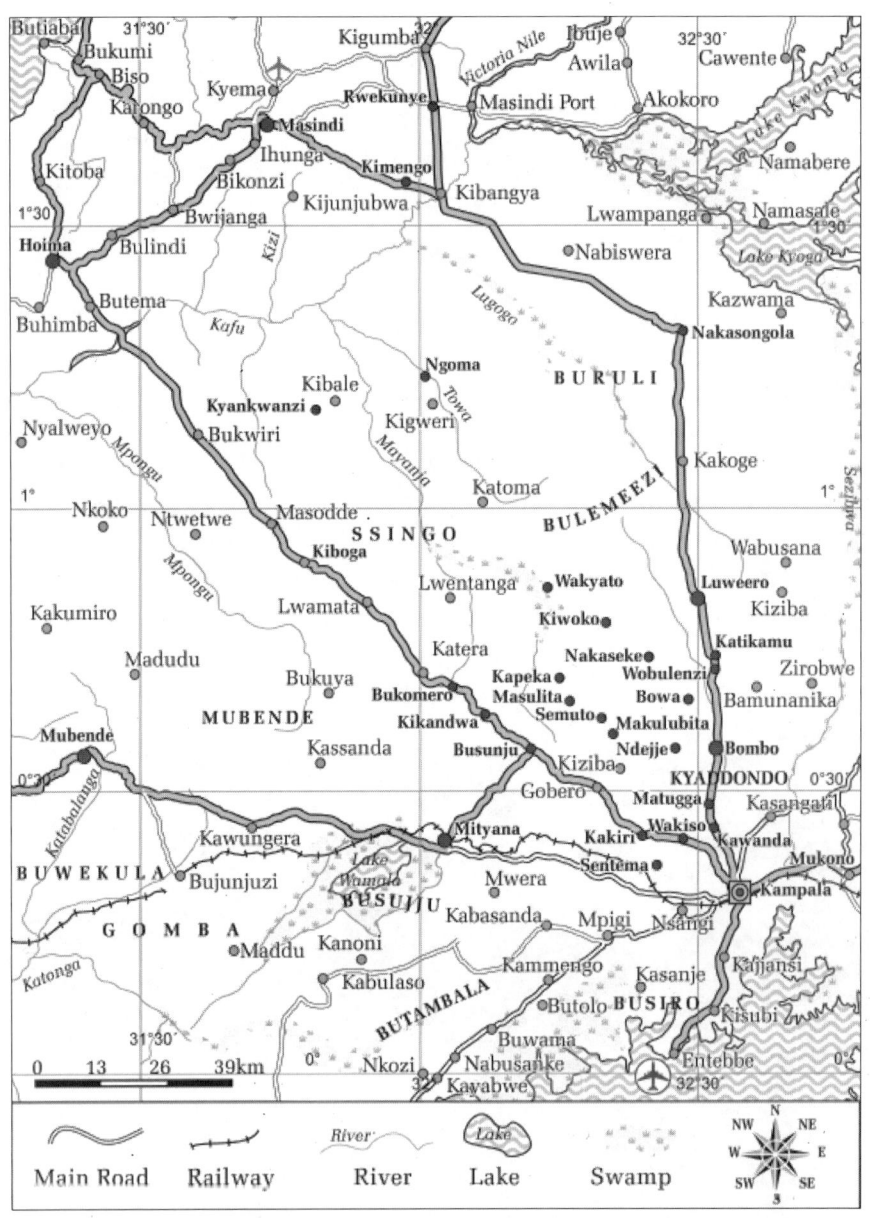

Map of Luwero Triangle, the nucleus of the resistance war 1981-1986

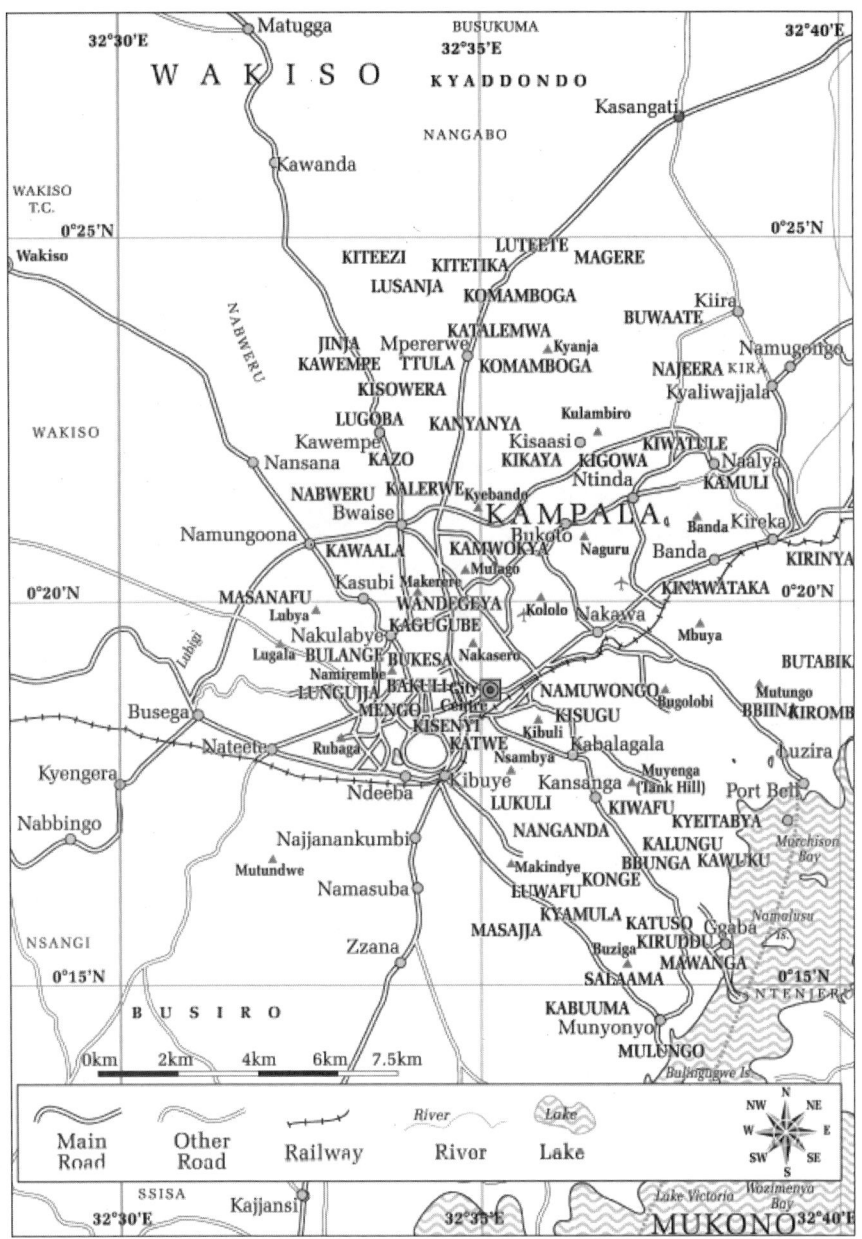

Map of Kampala

1

Is there an African Way of War?

'A man chosen to wield life and death on the battlefield must be an artist, if he isn't, he is simply a murderer.'
                                                            Shaka Zulu

One of the first history articles I remember reading as a freshman at the Command and General Staff College (Fort Leavenworth), was the *'The Western Way of War'* by Geoffrey Parker. This paper identified four elements as distinctive of the sort of warfare practised by western European states and their North American extension. These were: a reliance on technology; military discipline; a continuing military tradition (sustained by the practice of recording military events); and a challenge-response dynamic (a complex concept; but essentially Parker meant the history of competition between western European states, in terms of the technology of war. Also, the sophisticated financial systems, that allowed them to pay for this technological progress). These were the aspects of warfare in western Europe that eventually allowed that part of the world to conquer (for a time at least) much of the globe.

In addition, one could mention the western obsession with battles of decision. This in practical terms conveyed the glorification of battles of furious destruction; that would lead to the unconditional surrender of enemies. In the words of Geoffrey Parker, 'As Carl von Clausewitz put it in his early nineteenth-century treatise *On War*: The direct annihilation of the enemy's forces must always be the dominant consideration because destruction of the enemy forces is the overriding principle of war...'. Many classical writers commented on the utter ruthlessness of hoplites and legionaries, and in the early modern period the phrase *bellum romanum* acquired the sense of 'war without mercy' and became the standard military technique of Europeans abroad'[1]. Indeed, from King Leonidas's famous last stand at Thermopylae in 480 B.C.(where 300 Spartans killed 20,000 Persians before being butchered themselves) to the second battle of Falluja in Iraq in 2004, the western fixation with the physical destruction of the enemy is unmistakable.

The Oriental system of warfare (and this essentially means warfare as practised by the two great powers of the Orient in history, i.e. China and Japan) was more subtle but every bit as lethal. Preferring the indirect approach to warfare, the Oriental system extolled maneuver above the physical destruction of the enemy's mass. By relying on deception, cunning, pre-emption, speed and by attacking vulnerabilities the ancients of the east overcame adversaries. Sun Tzu, the ancient Chinese military sage had counselled that, 'For to win one hundred victories in one hundred battles is not the acme of skill. To subdue the enemy without fighting is the acme of skill'[2]. In other words, Sun Tzu reasoned that to defeat an enemy without having to shed blood was the supreme mark of good generalship. Therefore, the Oriental system put a premium on maneuver.

One of the best definitions of maneuver was proposed by Robert Leonhard in his seminal book *The Art of Maneuver*. He describes maneuver as '[attempting] to defeat the enemy through means other than simple destruction of his mass'[3]. Leonhard goes on to identify three ways maneuver has commonly been achieved throughout military history. These means are: *pre-emption, dislocation*, and *disruption*. Pre-emption should be understood as 'seizing an opportunity before the enemy does'[4], and normally requires early resolve in the mind of the commander and preternatural speed in execution. Essentially, pre-emption amounts to nipping a critical situation in the bud, it catches the enemy flat-footed and usually engenders revulsion from those who don't understand it.

'Dislocation' means to render ineffective the enemy's strength. If you can prevent the enemy from bringing superior forces to bear against you at a time and place of your choosing then you have dislocated him. We shall see that the National Resistance Army (NRA) utilized *positional* dislocation in the resistance war as a means of defeating the UNLA.

'Disruption' is the third instrument of maneuver and should be understood as 'the practice of defeating the enemy by attacking his center of gravity'[5]. Both friendly forces and the enemy have centers of gravity, located at all the levels of war (strategic, operational and tactical). In essence, a center of gravity is the enemy's (or our own) source of strength that contains within it a critical vulnerability (an Achilles heel). Attack this critical vulnerability and the enemy's stamina collapses. Destroying or neutralizing the enemy's source of strength will paralyze him. In the words of Leonhard, 'The aim of disruption then, is to avoid having to physically destroy the entire physical component of the enemy force by direct attack, in favor of rendering it inert by discerning and attacking its Achilles' heel'[6].

If Occidental military culture was biased towards decisive battles of annihilation and Oriental martial experience towards maneuver, was there an African theme to warfare? If so what was it? And can we discern it amidst the rifle fire and the thunder of artillery shells that serenaded the Ugandan resistance war?

Any attempt at scrutiny of the 'African way of war' instantly runs into the complication of trying to reduce the vast African experience with warfare into an easily comprehensible description. Was it biased towards maneuver or was it concerned with the annihilation of the opposition? Africa is vast and throughout history (both recorded and oral) has produced a variety of approaches to warfare. Therefore, just like any analysis of the Oriental way of war is chiefly concerned with warfare as practiced by a few principal states in antiquity, I shall limit my foray into this subject to an examination of the practices of three states. The first two, Ethiopia and the Zulu Empire represent powerful trends in the military history of the continent. Indeed, in some ways these two cases could be representative of the entire continent. The third is Ankole, any effort at understanding the underlying culture and attitude towards warfare of the NRA must of necessity be cognizant of the military traditions of Ankole. A majority of the principal commanders of the NRA were from territories associated with the Kingdom of Ankole (which was in essence a conglomeration of formerly disparate but related entities) and had therefore been schooled in the conventions of the Banyankore (people of Ankole). Their peasant upbringing in this part of Uganda prompted them to consciously or unconsciously incorporate these viewpoints into the conduct of the resistance war. Undoubtedly, Yoweri Museveni (the

Commander-in-Chief of the resistance forces) was heavily influenced by the customs and predilections of the Banyankore.

Ethiopian civilization can be traced back to 1000 B.C. In the first century B.C. Aksum (predecessor to modern Ethiopia) along with Rome, Persia and China were considered to be the four great powers of the age. By the third century A.D. Christianity had become the official religion of Aksum. Aksum expanded to include all of modern day Yemen, southern Arabia, southern Egypt, northern Sudan, northern Ethiopia, Eritrea, Djibouti, and northern Somalia. At the time of the European expansion into the continent, Ethiopia had recovered from a period of warlordism (1755-1855); this renaissance period is known as 'Zemene Misafint' (Age of Princes) and it began with the rule of Emperor Tewodros II in 1855. By the time of the decisive battle of Adowa in 1896, the power of the Emperor (which had waned during the warlord era) had been completely restored.

On 1st March 1896, Emperor Menelik II led his 80,000 Ethiopians to an overwhelming victory over an army of 17,700 Italians commanded by General Oreste Baratieri. In a battle of annihilation fought over the course of that day in the hills and valley of Adowa 7,000 Italians were massacred, 1,500 were wounded and 3,000 captured as prisoners of war. By mid-day on the 1st of March 1896 the remnants of the once proud Italian army were in full retreat, scurrying back to Eritrea. The battle of Adowa is one of the central events in modern African military history. It not only ensured the continued independence of an ancient African state, it also overturned the racial theories at the heart of colonialism. Indeed, Adowa was not only an immensely important African event but a world event of massive significance. It proclaimed that it was possible for a non-European entity to decisively beat a European power and would remain a powerful symbol for the anti-colonial movement throughout the globe for decades to come.

There can be little doubt that the Ethiopian victory at Adowa was a battle of decision in the tradition of the Western way of war. Menelik II's Ethiopian army was composed of riflemen, but also of infantry and cavalry armed only with spears. However, through an adept use of terrain and aggressive tactics they decimated an army that had superior technology. The battle was characterized by relentless Ethiopian mass attacks and the devastating charges of Menelik's Oromo cavalry, that slaughtered an entire Italian brigade.

The Zulu of southern Africa on the other hand had no cavalry. By 1816 (the year of Shaka's rise to power) this martial nation drew its strength from its incomparable infantry. The Zulu were a relatively small clan in service of the larger Mthetwa clan. Shaka was the son of Chief Senzangakhona of the Zulus and Nandi daughter of the Elangeni tribe. Shaka was probably conceived out of wedlock. He spent his childhood with his mother's people and as a teenager was initiated into the regiments of Chief Dingiswayo, an exiled prince of the Mthetwa. He probably served 10 years in Mthetwa formations and developed into a first class warrior. Shaka and Dingiswayo developed a close working relationship and in many ways Dingiswayo was Shaka's mentor. At the death of his father in 1816, Shaka aided by Dingiswayo took control of the Zulu. The two warrior chiefs forged an alliance of their peoples, although Dingiswayo remained the senior partner in this coalition.

Some years later Dingiswayo was killed in an ambush by the Ndwandwe, a powerful people from the north. Shaka united the Zulu and Mthetwa and made it his personal mission to avenge

Dingiswayo's blood. In a long running conflict Shaka's forces were eventually able to defeat the Ndwandwe and their warrior chief Zwide at the battles of Gqokli Hill (near the Mfolozi river), and later in a two-day running battle near Mhlautze river. Shaka then personally led a force to destroy Zwide's royal kraal. The erstwhile powerful warrior chief of the Ndwandwe escaped with a few followers but soon died in unclear circumstances. By the time he was assassinated in 1828 (at the hands of jealous brothers), Shaka ruled over 250,000 people and could muster an army of 50,000 warriors. His power was such that Portuguese traders in Mozambique paid tribute to him.

Prior to Shaka's rise, warfare in southern Africa (between the Tukhela and Phongolo rivers) had involved hardly any fighting. It comprised of a 'ritualized exchange of taunts with minimal loss of life'[7]. This ritualization of warfare was similar in certain regards to the 'flower wars' between the Aztecs (of Mexico) and the tribes that bordered them. Aztec warfare was based on a sort of agreement meant to provide the Aztec god Huitzicoatl with human blood (this was because a majority of these tribes essentially believed in the same gods). In the words of Robert Leonhard, 'Once challenge had been officially offered, priests from either side would meet to arrange for battle on the most auspicious day. Each side was meticulous about giving the enemy the best opportunity to prepare for the battle'[8]. The victorious side in the 'flower wars' would focus on capturing enough manpower in order to offer them in sacrifice to Huitzicoatl. The 'flower wars' were bloody affairs but for reasons other than the quick and efficient subjugation of the enemy.

Similarly, warfare between the different clans in southern Africa was based on an unwritten code that (in this case) abhorred bloodshed.

Unlike the Aztecs, warfare in southern Africa was not meant to serve religious obligations. Battles were preceded by sessions of verbal jousting, in which insults were hurled at the opposition. Then spears would be thrown at the enemy until one side surrendered. Sometimes the issue was decided by a fight between champions, the champion who won, would win the day for his clan and chief.

Shaka shattered this consensus. Warfare was meant to ensure the physical destruction of the enemy, in Shaka's mind. He is said to have told Dingiswayo, 'Strike an enemy once and for all. Let him cease to exist as a tribe or he will live to fly at your throat again'[9]. It is evident that Shaka was a forceful practitioner and advocate of battles of annihilation. He introduced measures that pretty soon swept aside the old methods of warfare. These included the short stabbing spear (*iklwa*), a large shield (which was used to hook the enemy's shield to the side thus exposing the ribs for a fatal thrust by the *iklwa*), sandal free feet, rigorous conditioning of men through forced marches, and cow-horn tactics. With these innovations Shaka revolutionized warfare in southern Africa. His conquests led to the migrations of hundreds of thousands, all attempting to escape the great warrior's warpath. This period of great upheaval in southern Africa is known as the 'Mfecane' and its impact was felt as far afield as East Africa with the arrival of the Ngoni in Tanzania.

On 22nd January 1879, a superbly armed British force of about 4,000 under Lord Chelmsford encountered a Zulu army numbering about 24,000 at Isandhlwana. The British had instigated the war in order to decisively beat the Zulu and bring them into submission. The Zulu were led by Cetshwayo (a nephew of Shaka) and demonstrated all their fabled military skills in the battle of Isandhlwana. Lord Chelmsford was dismissive of Zulu military prowess and walked straight into Cetshwayo's ingeniously designed stratagem. He was lured into splitting his force, personally leading the bulk of his men to meet a perceived advance by the Zulu main force. He left 1,400 men under Lieutenant Colonel Henry Pulleine back at the camp at Isandhlwana. While Chelmsford raced to meet only a portion of the Zulu force (about 4,000 warriors), the main Zulu army had out maneuvered him. On the morning of 22nd January 1879, a troop of British scouts discovered this massive force of 20,000 warriors seated in total silence in a valley right next to the British camp. The Zulus attacked without hesitation driving all before them. By 3:00 pm that afternoon, the camp had been overrun and 1,327 men had lost their lives on the British side (this includes British regulars and their local cohorts). Lord Chelmsford returned to an utterly devastated camp, and to the humiliation of having presided over the worst military defeat ever to befall a British colonial army by an indigenous force.

The area that came to be known as Ankole at the start of the colonial era included Nkore and the quasi-independent principalities of Mpororo. These states had been part of the Chwezi Empire that had endured for 600 years (from 900 AD to 1500 AD). The Chwezi Empire embraced all of present day Uganda, parts of eastern DRC, Rwanda and north-western Tanzania. After the collapse of the glorious Chwezi, a number of smaller successor states emerged to fill the vacuum left by the great empire. These were the inter-lacustrine kingdoms of Bunyoro, Buganda, Nkore, Mpororo, Karagwe, Rwanda and Burundi. The ruling dynasties in these new states all claimed blood relations with the Chwezi. The ruling dynasty of Bunyoro, the Babito were supposed to be the offspring of Chwezi fathers and women from 'Buciri,' what we now call Lango. The ruling dynasty in Nkore (the Bahinda), were the offspring of the Chwezi by Ruhinda, son of Wamara (last emperor of the Chwezi) and Njunaki (one of his maids). The ancient rulers of Karagwe, Bujinja and Buha all claim Ruhinda as a founding father. In other words Ruhinda is the forebear of the Banyankore (of Nkore-Mpororo), Banyambo (of Karagwe), Bahaya (of Bukoba), Bashubi and Baha (of Kigoma).

Early warfare in Ankole seemed to be characterized by engagements where heroes would decide the issue. An example is the giant *'Muguta ya Butaaho Eshungyera Nigachweka'* (Muguta son of Butaaho, who soars over clashing spears), the fabled hero of Buhweju, whose legendary exploits live on to this day. Muguta probably lived at the turn of the 17th Century and was the leading warrior of Buhweju's king Kabundami II. Kabundami II instituted a special unit of warriors called *'Enkondami'* to protect him from the aggressions of Bunyoro. Muguta was the foremost warrior of the Nkondami. Legend tells of the titanic struggle between Muguta and Nkore's champion *'Ntsinga Embwa Ebambaire'* (Ntsinga the mad dog), at Rwebikoona (where Mbarara market stands today) over the theft of Kabundami II's favorite cow *'Mayenje ga Ishinjo'* by two famous thieves of Nkore. The two heroes displayed feats of supernatural strength leaping at each other as if untouched by gravity, Muguta managed to thrust his spear through an airborne *Ntsinga*, but in his agony *Ntsinga* fell upon the giant, sinking his teeth into his scalp and his fingers into his jugular vein. Try as he might Muguta could not release himself from *Ntsinga*'s deadly grip, the other *Nkondami* of Buhweju (who were present) could not come to Muguta's aid because culture prohibited unfair fights, which were looked upon with disdain. In Runyankore, this act of ganging up against one warrior in a fight is called *'okukombera'*. The *Nkondami* knew that their beloved giant-hero would seethe with rage if they committed this unthinkable indignity. The struggle between these two heroes ended in a draw and Kabundami II's beloved cow was returned to Buhweju.

By the time of Mutambuka's accession to the throne (probably around 1840) there had been a marked progression in warfare. Warfare in Nkore was no longer a matter for champions alone, standing regiments known as *emitwe* now enforced the monarch's writ throughout the kingdom and beyond. One regiment (*omutwe*) was composed of between 600-1000 warriors. Several regiments were known as *emigogo* and were often led by a general (usually a prince) trusted by the monarch.

Historically, military activity in Nkore had revolved around raids for cattle. Cattle ownership in Nkore and Mpororo was 'the only index of wealth'[10] and was therefore something to be greatly treasured. Territorial expansion started becoming a driving factor for wars with the accession of Mutambuka to the throne of Nkore. This was probably caused by social forces (like an expanded population), but also by the waning power of some of Nkore's powerful neighbours like Bunyoro. Bunyoro was increasingly unable to exercise effective control over territories adjacent to her. Additionally, Bunyoro was also constrained to utilize whatever strength it had left in its confrontation with its age old nemesis Buganda. Mutambuka's martial character contributed to these wars of territorial acquisition. Mutambuka's regiments were able to subdue the independent chieftaincies of Buhweju, Igara, Bunyaruguru, and Busongora (also called Makara).

The effect of these social changes (and changes in the balance of power) upon the practice of warfare was manifest. Although the formation of *emitwe* had started in the reign of Mutambuka's grandfather Rwebishengye, it was Mutambuka and his grandson

Ntare V who professionalized them. Warriors would be selected at an early age by the monarch and then get commissioned into a regiment. Regiments were always built around one of the king's herds, so that the function of these warriors was to tend the herd as well as receive military training. Normally, the leader of a regiment was one of the warriors in whom the monarch observed promise or a prince of the royal house who was in the same age bracket as most of the warriors in the regiment. Military training consisted of wrestling (*okufukaana*), drills with spear and shield, as well as archery (*okumaasha*). These drills were often carried out concurrently with herding (usually when not engaged in watering the cows or prodding them to move to better pasture).

The leader of the *omutwe* fused both military and civil responsibilities in the area in which his unit was located. Indeed, he was a military governor of sorts in that locality; he would dispense justice in the name of the king to the inhabitants of his region. The regimental leader had the authority to launch raids in order to capture cattle without reference to the monarch. However, it seems military operations meant to annex territory were always planned by the monarch and entrusted to his foremost general.

For much of Mutambuka's reign the foremost general was Bacwa (the king's eldest son), he was beloved of his father and the army. Through this remarkable warrior Nkore struck terror into the hearts of its neighbors. However, Bacwa was destined never to succeed his father on account of the envy and loathing of his paternal aunt – Kibangura. The story of Bacwa and Kibangura is a fascinating one but not the focus of this study; suffice to say that because Bacwa did not succeed his father, one of the bitterest succession wars in Nkore ensued. This succession war was essentially between Bacwa loyalists and allies of Kibangura. By treachery, the ranks of Bacwa's followers (other sons of Mutambuka) were decimated until eventually they were led by his young son Ntare.

The story of Ntare's rise to power (through the succession war) is remarkable not least because of its uncanny resemblance to the NRA resistance war. The civil war between the princes of Nkore lasted about three years (from about 1867 – 1870), it was a protracted struggle. Ntare's side started off much weaker than the opposition (which was led by Mukwenda and Muhikira) and the young prince adopted more or less a guerrilla strategy. Ntare avoided decisive battles and concentrated on the survival of his small band of followers. His side enjoyed massive public support because Ntare was Bacwa's son, but also because most people were aghast at the treachery of Mukwenda and Kibangura.

This popularity served to recruit more fighters to Ntare's cause and consequently strengthen him. By 1870, Ntare felt strong enough to stand and fight his adversaries on the field of battle. The battle of Mugoye in present day Kanoni County (Kiruhura District) was a decisive engagement. Both Mukwenda and Muhikira were killed in the fierce fighting and Ntare (who assumed the regal name of Ntare V) was victorious.

It is important to note here that this senseless fratricide on the part of the ruling dynasties of most of the kingdoms of the interlacustrine region, helps explain the weakened state which European imperialism found these polities in. The people of these states were a powerful martial race, but their leaders were deficient in the foresight and good judgment to unite them and keep them that way. These societies were fractured and ruled by selfish, autocratic monarchs. Ultimately, they were overthrown on account of these reckless leaders.

All three illustrations reveal that warfare in east and southern Africa was certainly progressing down the road of the western way of war. Warfare was transforming (as in the case of the Zulu empire and Nkore) and battles of annihilation were becoming the dominant form of conflict. However, the genius of Ntare V of Nkore had introduced maneuver to the battlefields of south-western Uganda during the succession war. Ntare V was later to utilize maneuver warfare against the Rwandese invasion of 1894 scoring a massive victory against that power.

In the succession war, Ntare V initially 'dislocated' the armies of Mukwenda by constantly avoiding decisive battles; he made it impossible for Mukwenda to bring his greater strength to bear against his inferior forces. Utilizing what would later be called Maoist methods, Ntare V 'traded space for time'. In other words Ntare V did not hesitate to give ground if he thought it would buy time to build on his strength. Ntare V's system of warfare would be replicated by the NRA (consciously or unconsciously) although for all intents and purposes, Yoweri Museveni (the guiding military theorist of the resistance) genuflected to Mao Zedong, and considered his doctrine pertinent to the progression of the war.

In conclusion, it would seem that there is indeed a unique and innate African way of war, which is a product of the specific history and peculiarities of the continent. The fact that this variant of warfare has certain similarities to other models says something about the relative continuity in the development of warfare by the human race, regardless of location. In eastern and southern Africa, battles of decision (or battles of slaughter) were emerging as the dominant and preferred method of fighting. For large, sophisticated and ancient states like Ethiopia this form of warfare had evolved sufficiently to bring to a screeching halt the colonial ambitions of a major western power, something that only Japan (apart from Ethiopia) managed to achieve in the whole of the non-European world. In southern Africa, the successors of Shaka the Great utilizing a decisive battle were able to humble the greatest imperial power in all of human history, proving that Africans were not lacking in warrior ethos and were every bit the soldiers that their better equipped opposition were. Finally, in Nkore the trend towards battles of annihilation continued unabated, however, Ntare V deviated from this, pressed by the exigencies of a civil war in which his side was at a disadvantage. He stumbled upon 'maneuver warfare' and in a brilliant military campaign that foreshadowed the Ugandan resistance war he enriched the African way of war.

Notes

1. Geoffrey Parker, *The Western Way of War*, http://assets.cambridge.org/9780521853590/excerpt/9780521853590_excerpt.pdf accessed August 15 2008.
2. Sun Tzu, *The Art of War*,
3. Robert Leonhard, *The Art of Maneuver*, Maneuver-Warfare Theory and Airland Battle, (New York, Ballantine Publishing Group, 1991), 19.
4. Robert Leonhard, *The Art of Maneuver*, Maneuver-Warfare Theory and Airland Battle, (New York, Ballantine Publishing Group, 1991), 62.
5. Robert Leonhard, *The Art of Maneuver*, (New York, Ballantine Publishing Group, 1991) 73.
6. Robert Leonhard, *The Art of Maneuver*, (New York, Ballantine Publishing Group, 1991) 73.
7. Shaka, Wikipedia the Free Encyclopedia, http://en.wikipedia.org/wiki/Shaka_Zulu#Shaka.27s_social_and_military_revolution accessed August 19 2008
8. Robert Leonhard, *The Art of Maneuver*, (New York, Ballantine Publishing Group, 1991) 3.
9. Military Quotes/Quotations, http://www.military-quotes.com/database/z.htm accessed August 19 2008
10. Samwiri Rubaraza Karugire, *A History of the Kingdom of Nkore in Western Uganda to 1896*, (Kampala, Fountain Publishers Ltd, 2007), 206

2

Mbale 1973: 'Cometh the Hour, Cometh the Man'

'When forces of oppression come to maintain themselves in power against established law, peace is considered already broken'.
                                                    Che Guevara

Occasionally, in the history of a nation, a people, a struggle, or an army, a particular place, an individual locale, acquires historic importance that surpasses any native qualities that it seemingly presents. Somebody once said that 'war was God's way of teaching us geography'. What immortalizes places like Cannae, Austerlitz, Waterloo, Gettysburg, Sedan and Isandhlwana? Or places like Eban Emael, Cabanatuan and the old terminal building at Entebbe? Invariably it is the events that took place there. Somehow these violent human experiences affect the aura of the places they occurred in, the anguished emotions of the participants and their supreme sacrifice imbues the soil with mysticism. The Ugandan nation is well provisioned with such hallowed ground.

Located in the south-east of Uganda is the town of Mbale. Mbale is situated in the shadow of the imposing Elgon massif. In the north-western portion of that municipality is Maluku Estate, a plain and unembellished housing estate back in 1973. Mbale town is 190 kilometres from Kampala in the north-easterly direction, in 1973 it was a charming and clean little town. The Bagisu people of Mbale district cultivated millet, potatoes, beans and simsim as food crops (for subsistence consumption). They grew coffee and cotton for commercial purposes. The social structure of the district at the time, like most of the rest of the country, positioned a small group of educated (and quasi-educated) municipal leaders, professionals and traders on top of the majority peasant farmers. In early 1973 when the Maluku Estate episode took place Idi Amin (Uganda's military dictator who had seized control of the country in 1971) had just expelled the Asian community. The existence of an Asian community in Uganda had been a result of the British colonial government's policies. The Asians supported by the colonialists had controlled most of the trade in the country. Amin's coup d'état had initially been welcomed by those whose distaste for Uganda's first prime-minister Milton Obote, was so overpowering that they were unable to detect the similarities in the two men. The truth was that Amin was the brutal executioner of Obote's craftily designed schemes; those who anticipated positive changes with Amin's seizure of power were all too soon bitterly disappointed.

Yoweri Museveni had come into contact with Maumbe Mukwana around 1970. Both had been members of the Uganda Vietnam Solidarity Committee (UVSC) which had been formed by Dani Wadada Nabudere (a lawyer who had a private practice in Mbale) in the late 1960s. UVSC was created to express support for the people of Vietnam and their nationalist struggle for self-determination. Maumbe had worked as a municipal councillor in Mbale before Amin's seizure of power; after that, he had lost his job because the dictator had abolished elected local government councils and taken to appointing local leaders.

Museveni's leftist credentials had been sufficiently advertised by his spirited involvement in the student politics at the University of Dar es Salaam in the 1960s. The University of Dar es Salaam, inspired by the patriotic and nationalist politics of *'Mwalimu'* Julius Nyerere had evolved into the focus of radical student activism within East Africa. Museveni had been at the center of this radicalism and had used his considerable personal charisma to popularize the student movement in Tanzania. Museveni's energy and militancy soon became part of the folklore of the university, with deferential students referring to him as *'mwana chama halisi'* (a complete/genuine party member). Julius Nyerere was drawn to Museveni's radical brand of politics as indeed were other elements in the Nyerere administration.

Maumbe remembers reading about Museveni in the monthly newsletters at the Soviet Embassy in Kampala long before he met him. Museveni's activities in support of liberation movements in southern Africa (like FRELIMO of Mozambique) were a regular news item in the gazettes of the Uganda Soviet Friendship Society (USFS). Maumbe's own journey to leftist politics had been initiated by his expulsion from UPC by Milton Obote at the 1964 Gulu Delegates Conference. His crime had been that he was accompanied to the conference by a black American lady whom he was dating at the time (this at any rate was one of the pretexts used to remove him from UPC). Obote alleged that Maumbe was a CIA agent (because of his affair with the American woman) and this enraged the proud young man. Obote's real motivation was his struggle for paramount power within UPC and his fear of John Kakonge - UPC's charismatic Secretary General. Maumbe had been identified as an enthusiastic and unrepentant friend of

John Kakonge by the Obote faction in UPC. John Kakonge was removed from the position of Secretary General of the UPC at the same delegates conference. With his pride wounded and now without a political party, an embittered Maumbe decided to plunge into the politics of the radical left in retaliation at the UPC and Obote that he perceived as, at best, tepid leftists.

The surge of nationalist fervor that engulfed the African continent as part of decolonization in the late 1950s and throughout the 1960s up until the mid 1970s, lent itself very much to leftism. In reality, the oppressed peoples of Africa and Asia used the international contradictions between the capitalist west and communist east to purchase their freedom. African nationalists were not inherently opposed to capitalism; they were against the capitalist west in so far as colonialism (that had robbed them of freedom and enslaved them) was inextricably linked to capitalism (or the sort of capitalism that subsisted then). Colonialism was an evil that was responsible for the death, enslavement, humiliation and degradation of hundreds of millions of human beings; it had to be utterly annihilated. In many African countries, it became fashionable (and indeed necessary) for prospective independence leaders to bedeck themselves in the garments of socialism. Association with the west was not something to aspire to; indeed, it was reserved for villains like Mobutu Sese Seko and Moise Tshombe. That was why people like Milton Obote, although by temperament and inclination essentially conservative, masqueraded as socialists.

Maumbe first saw Museveni in early 1970 outside the Ministry of Foreign Affairs building in Kampala. He was immediately impressed by Museveni; he also got the sense that the thin young man had done some military training. There was something about the way he carried himself that gave you the distinct feeling that he was a trained soldier', Maumbe recalled. Eventually, in late 1970 Museveni visited Maumbe in Mbale. It was just after Brigadier Okoya had been assassinated in Gulu, and Museveni was terse as he enquired what Maumbe thought of the situation in the country. Maumbe proceeded to give him his assessment and Museveni in his customary manner re-visited points that Maumbe had raised and re-interpreted issues that he thought were important. 'Here was this intense man who was five years younger than me indoctrinating me', Maumbe mused when the author interviewed him. After a few hours, Museveni stood up and took his leave. A few months later Major General Idi Amin Dada (the Army Commander) ousted Milton Obote.

Elizabeth (Beth) Mukwana (Maumbe's wife) remembers that her home at 49 Maluku Estate hosted the energetic Museveni on numerous occasions. Most of the time he was in the company of one or two other young men. They would have long, lively discussions with her husband for hours on end. Sometimes the young men would sleep over and she would prepare one of the two rooms in her humble house for them. Beth's younger brother Moses Mukholi who shared the room with the young men on those occasions remembers waking up in the wee hours and seeing the men still in animated discussion.

Beth did not get involved in the discussions between her husband and the young men; this would have been violation of the customs and traditions of the Bagisu. That was not her place and so she gave the men the space they needed. However, she could not help but notice that politics preponderated in their dialogue and that Museveni was always the most categorical of the group.

Beth did not give it much thought though; she presumed it was nothing more than young men letting off steam. The notion that it could be something serious never crossed her mind; her husband had labored to ensure that she was blissfully unaware of what he and his frequent visitors were actually doing.

Although of modest means, Beth's father had struggled to provide her with an education. Beth had managed to complete her O-levels and then qualified as a Grade III teacher; she did her teacher training at Kyambogo Government Teachers Training College. In early 1973, she was teaching at North Road Primary School in Mbale and her salary of 700 shillings supplemented the domestic revenues.

On the 22nd of January 1973 at around 5.00 pm, Beth returned home from work to find Yoweri Museveni, Martin Mwesiga and Kazimoto at her house. The three men were seated in a rudimentary sofa on the far end of the small living room, that was the first room one accessed from the front of the house. They were clearly exhausted and hungry. Museveni asked Beth to prepare some tea for them; she told him that she was fresh out of cash since it was almost the end of the month (Beth's teaching job paid her on the last day of the month). Museveni reached for his pocket and gave her a twenty shilling note and asked her to go to the market and buy whatever was needed to make tea for them. She walked out of the house through the back door (prior to exiting by way of this door one had to walk through a small kitchen). The back door ushered one to a back yard of sorts, the only difference was that there were no fences in Maluku Estate. Thus, a person could walk quite comfortably through the estate using the communal backyards as an avenue of egress or ingress. Beth had not walked far when she noticed a group of soldiers (maybe around ten) in the environs of the house. Three soldiers who seemed to be in the process of questioning someone caught her attention; before long the three men turned and started to walk in the direction of 49 Maluku Estate. Beth hurried back to let her guests know that something was afoot.

Patrick Bukeni, a relation of Maumbe Mukwana, as fate would decree, arrived at the house moments after Beth had left for the market. He worked with the East African Community in Arusha. He had crossed the Kenya-Uganda border that afternoon and proceeded to the Maumbe home as soon as he disembarked from his bus at Mbale Bus Park. He noticed the guests' white Volkswagen Beetle 1600 parked outside as he entered the house. Inside the house he sat down in a seat that was immediately adjacent to the front door. He was immediately engaged in conversation by a light skinned man of slight build who wore outdoor type boots. The man (Museveni) asked him a lot of questions, when Bukeni told him that he worked in Arusha; the man claimed that he knew that area very well having worked in Moshi as a teacher for some time. As Museveni spoke, Bukeni could not stop thinking about his boots, this was because in Uganda at that time people who wore military type boots were associated with the security forces in some way. What particularly concerned Bukeni was that he worked in Tanzania, a country that Amin's government had proscribed as a haven of dissident activity.* For all he knew he might be talking to one of Amin's intelligence operatives.

As Museveni continued to engage Bukeni, Maumbe's mother charged into the house from the direction of the kitchen. She was wailing and yelling something about 'her children going to

---

* In September 1972, Ugandan exiles based in Tanzania launched a poorly planned invasion of the country at the behest of Milton Obote. The disastrous adventure led to the death of hundreds of the exiles, and the souring of Uganda-Tanzania relations.

die'. She spoke to Bukeni in Lugisu telling him that soldiers were approaching the house (it is unclear whether Museveni and his comrades understood what was being communicated to Bukeni). At this point she ran back out of the house, Bukeni rushed after her without letting his interlocutors know what the fuss was about. Bukeni still operated under the belief that the men in his relation's lounge were in some way associated with the military and were responsible for this mess in the first place. Once outside, he saw soldiers converging on the house through the foliage; he turned to re-enter the house and pick up his briefcase which contained 800 dollars in traveller's cheques and identification papers.

The old woman who was hysterical by now grabbed his arm and told him to forget about the briefcase if he valued his life and get the hell out of there! Bukeni glanced in the direction that was opposite to where the soldiers seemed to be approaching from, he saw no one there and ran at full pelt.

By the time Beth got back to the house, a rumor had circulated that the soldiers were looking for a thief. She told her guests that she had seen soldiers in the neighborhood. A flurry of consultations took place between the three men, with Museveni arguing for a robust response to the threat and Mwesiga counseling that they should not overreact, that is, they should not make a bad situation worse. Mwesiga recommended that they should stick to the cover story (that they were using at that point) of being students and the soldiers would leave them alone.

Museveni's instinctive reaction to fight reveals his already developed insight (even at this early stage in his self-education in the art of war) into the nature of tactical engagements. From his autobiography- *Sowing the Mustard Seed* - we know that by 1973, Museveni and another comrade Valerian Rwaheru had already learnt to kill when the situation demanded it (e.g. on Kaluba road in 1972 or earlier in the attack on Mbarara on the 16th and 17th of September 1972). The trouble with clandestine operations of the sort that Museveni and his friends were engaged in, or what we might understand today as special operations or special missions, is correctly judging when the situation is so critical as to warrant violence. Of course, this judgment is tempered by how good an operative's cover story is; if the reasons that place you in a specific enemy locale are beyond reproach then you might consider a non-confrontational solution. Obviously, any security force worthy of mention would take a very dim view of anyone taking photographs of a military barracks (for example) whatever their bona fides. However, as a rule in special operations, one takes a very pessimistic attitude towards the enemy and from the start comes expecting a fight. In special operations, one prepares for the worst contingency and makes sure that when things go amiss regardless of small numbers the enemy will be made to pay for it. Cynicism keeps you alive in circumstances like these.

There is another element to Museveni's reaction that holds some instruction for the special operators of today. In deciding to fight (in spite of the odds stacked against him) Museveni demonstrated an innate appreciation of the idea of 'relative superiority' which is the cornerstone tenet of special operations. Relative superiority is described as 'a condition that exists when an attacking force, generally smaller, gains a decisive advantage over a larger or well-defended enemy'[11]. Relative superiority is achieved through a number of principles, that all Special Forces are familiar with, two of these are surprise and speed, both of which Museveni applied to the predicament he faced at 49 Maluku Estate.

We shall see in what manner this was achieved but before going any further, it is critical to explain that by acclaiming Museveni's actions in Mbale and in subsequent situations, we are not trying to elevate him to the status of Clausewitz's famous description of genius in war. Describing war as the realm of *danger, physical exertion, uncertainty and chance*, Clausewitz defined genius in war (or the 'sovereign eye of genius'[12], as he termed it) as 'gifts of mind and temperament that in combination bear on military activity'[13]. Clausewitz* proceeded to list these 'outstanding' and 'exceptional' gifts as *courage (physical and moral), a discerning intellect, determination, presence of mind and strength of character*. Although Museveni displayed all these qualities to some degree at Maluku Estate, the trouble with the Clausewitzian ideal of genius in war, is that it's just that- an ideal. It is a 'superlative degree of talent'[14] in Clausewitz's own words; it is supreme and unmatched talent which more often than not is noticeable by its absence in individuals than by its presence.

The taut discussion between the three men was brought to an abrupt end by a dark- skinned soldier who stood in the doorway and bawled orders to the occupants of the house. His first question was who was the owner of the white Volkswagen parked outside? Beth answered that it belonged to her guests. He then ordered her guests out of the house; the three men walked out of the house and stood in a line on the small veranda outside. They stood facing

---

*   Carl von Clausewitz (1780-1831) was a Prussian senior officer and military theorist, whose book *On War*, that was unfinished at the time of his death, is considered to be one of the greatest (if not the greatest) classics of the art of war. He was responsible for coining concepts like 'The Remarkable Trinity', 'Center of Gravity', 'Genius in War', 'Decisive Point','Friction','Fog of War' and 'Culmination'. Clausewtz is to the study of war what Isaac Newton is to physics, or what Adam Smith is to modern economics.

west; the Volkswagen was parked with its front looking south, therefore essentially Museveni, Mwesiga and Kazimoto stood in front of the house, on the balcony. In the small enclosure at the front of the house stood three soldiers, two of whom were armed with self loading rifles (SLRs).

The third soldier was of a lighter complexion and was stoutly built; he looked like he hailed from one of the districts in south-western Uganda. He wore a red sash indicating that he was a man of some authority, most probably a non-commissioned officer (NCO). He did not speak much and left much of the talking to the soldier who had ordered the men out of the house. Museveni turned and looked north and noticed that there were more soldiers on either side of the small asphalt road that ran through the estate; they seemed to be conducting some kind of sweep in a southerly direction. He estimated that they must have been around ten or twelve.

Museveni was standing closest to the dark soldier (who was probably of the Kakwa people of northwest Uganda) who was doing much of the yapping. The soldier asked the men who they were? They answered that they were students. At this point he inquired who had the keys of the car and Museveni answered that it was him. That was the end of the questioning, the soldier then ordered them to get in the car and follow them. This sudden end to the questioning and categorical command to enter the car and drive to the barracks satisfied Museveni that these soldiers did not buy the student story, but also that they probably knew who they were. Complicating matters further, when Museveni and his friends had entered the house earlier they had kept their rifles in the car, the guns were still in the car and the soldiers would see them once it was opened.

As he commanded them to get in the car, he thrust the muzzle of his gun into Museveni's side indicating that he should get going. Museveni walked forward with one hand in his pocket as if he was trying to reach for the car keys. In order to access the driver's seat he had to walk right round the car. When he got behind the car (i.e. around the car's trunk) he leapt over the small hedge that delineated the front yard and bolted. For a moment there was commotion in the front yard; then the dark-skinned soldier gave chase. Mwesiga and Kazimoto were ordered by the NCO to kneel down in the front yard, with the third soldier training his gun at them.

Running like the wind with the Kakwa soldier in dogged pursuit, Museveni streaked in the direction of a eucalyptus forest. The soldier fired a volley of shots in Museveni's direction, but they were wide off the mark and Museveni kept going. Once he heard the shots, Museveni altered the way he was running, instead of racing in a straight line he started darting here and there in a zigzag fashion, which made him a much more difficult target. Residents of the estate who had been roused by the presence of soldiers and by the shooting tried to intercept Museveni, taking him for the thief that had been rumored to be in the neighbourhood. He pulled out the pistol that he had strapped to his belt and brandished it and they scampered. The soldier who was increasingly incensed by the pursuit and the fact that none of his shots hit home, fired more wildly hoping that one bullet would at the minimum disable Museveni. As bullets zipped around him, Museveni decided to give his pursuer something to think about. He found a large tree and using it for cover let off a couple of rounds with his pistol, one of his bullets hit the soldier in one of his arms. He shrieked in pain and fell to the ground.

Museveni entered a thicket of very tall grass; in later years he was to reminisce about the difficulty he encountered trying to traverse those few hundred meters of very thick bush. In *Sowing the Mustard Seed* he writes, 'Struggling with the tall grass was so difficult that if Amin's cowardly, bullying soldiers had had the courage to pursue me, I would have been an easy target…I shall never forget those 300 meters or so of tall grass through which I crashed my way. The odds were squarely stacked against me. I was moving very slowly through the tall thick grass, leaving a clear track which any pursuer could have followed. I was also growing very tired'[15]. What is not conveyed very clearly in the passage above is the very real sense of despair (the sense of 'helplessness' in his words) he felt as he thrashed about the bush. He cut a very lonely and wretched figure in the middle of that thick undergrowth; he must have wondered if that was it, if he was destined to perish in that unforgiving vegetation. All it took were a couple of enraged soldiers to take up the hunt once more to avenge their friend. The injured soldier now used his good arm to prop the arm that had been shattered by Museveni's well aimed fire and walked back to the compound in agony.

When Museveni jumped over the hedge back at the house, he had anticipated that his friends would take that occasion to disperse as well. Both Mwesiga and Kazimoto were Museveni's equal in terms of clandestine experience. Mwesiga was a very close and dear childhood friend of Museveni. He had been present at Kaluba road near Maga Maga when Valerian Rwaheru and Museveni killed a soldier who was trying to question them on their activities. Still at Kaluba road, Museveni had driven over the same soldier when his body somehow got entangled in their car's undercarriage. He was, therefore, aware of how Museveni might react when threatened. Kazimoto was another seasoned operator; Maumbe remembered how he organized the relocation of about seventeen armed fighters from a forest in Busoga to Busiu in Mbale. Maumbe recalled that Kazimoto did not speak much but was calm and confident. Maumbe did the driving and Kazimoto sat in the front passenger seat, when they got to Mbale, Kazimoto guided Maumbe to his own farm house in Busiu. Maumbe wasn't even aware that Kazimoto knew where his farm was, he was very surprised. When Maumbe tried to ask that the fighters be accommodated somewhere else, Kazimoto quietly but firmly refused his suggestions.

Mwesiga and Kazimoto had remained inert when Museveni bolted. They probably expected that he wouldn't make it, that he would be killed by all the soldiers that they could see around them. They probably imagined that they might have slightly better odds if they entered the car, maybe they might overpower the few soldiers they would sit with in the Volkswagen. Wielding rifles within the tight confines of the vehicle would have been difficult for the soldiers, and they probably visualized a close quarter's fist fight in the car. Even if the car had swerved off the road as a result of the scrap going on inside, the chances of surviving such an accident were better than the tender mercies they could expect from Amin's soldiers in a barracks. We will never know what those heroic men felt and thought in the final moments of their lives; all we can be certain of is that they maintained a valiant spirit to the last.

At some point when Museveni was still being chased by the Kakwa soldier, the non-commissioned officer (the soldier with the red sash) asked the two men who were kneeling in the front yard of the house why their friend was running. Mwesiga responded that he did not know why he was running. Beth recalls that a few minutes went by during which gunfire could be heard in the distance, after some time the soldier who had run after Museveni staggered back into the compound cradling his bleeding arm with his good arm. He was obviously in agony and whimpered *'mujama ame ni piga'* (the fellow has shot me). At which point the NCO ordered the soldier who had been aiming his rifle at the two men to fire. The shots that were fired felled Mwesiga and Kazimoto; Beth who was still standing in the doorway screamed and fled after she heard the shots and saw the two men fall to the ground.

Museveni recalls hearing shots coming from the direction of the estate as he was entering the eucalyptus forest that had been his goal when he first escaped from the house. He did not think much about it then (thinking these were the wild shots of his pursuers) and only learnt later that these were the shots that murdered his friends. After a titanic effort he had managed to get out of the thick bush and then ran along a drainage channel with the 'lightness and energy of an antelope', he told the author. He veered off the drainage channel and entered the forest at which point he heard the shots. He walked through the copse swiftly, after about twenty minutes he reached a banana plantation that was near a settlement. As he walked through the banana plantation, he could hear a large group of soldiers searching the thick bush through which he had struggled minutes earlier.

Eventually, he emerged on the main road to Bugema. It was now getting dark and Museveni in his usual derring-do manner decided to walk back to Mbale and find out what had happened to his friends. He chanced upon a young man who advised strongly against proceeding to Mbale. When Museveni asked what the reason for this was, the young man related what had transpired in town that day; he reported that two soldiers and two guerrillas had been killed. Amin's soldiers, he narrated, were on edge as a result, they were looking for any excuse to brutalize the population. This was when Museveni learnt of the death of his comrades and the news upset him profoundly.

His sorrow soon turned into a controlled rage that very nearly bordered on reckless courage. He wanted to kick himself for not having been more assertive with his friends, at the house. His face grimaced as he thought of how he should have ordered his colleagues to fight and not have brooked any debate.

After receiving this saddening news, Museveni walked with the boy to Bugema where he spent the night in a lodge. The following day he managed to travel all the way to Kampala. At Jinja he hopped into a Peugeot 404 taxi. There were another six or seven passengers in the same taxi. When they got to Namanve, the taxi came to a halt at a massive vehicle checkpoint. They were all ordered out by a stern looking soldier, who started questioning the occupants of the taxi. Once he disembarked, Museveni noticed that the checkpoint was manned by about a company of infantry; a few of them were actually on the road (about a section) and the rest were in the bush to one side of the road (most lying in the prone position with their rifles trained on the road). Still armed with a pistol and in a rage, Museveni was ready to take on the entire company. When the soldier got to him, an unflinching Museveni looked directly at the man as he responded to his questions. The soldier asked what he did and Museveni answered that he was a student, still focussed directly on the man's eyes. Sensing that there was something eerie about this man, the soldier did not ask anymore questions, but told Museveni to get back into the car. In later years, Museveni was to relate this story and tell of how he intended to shoot the man, take his rifle and run into the bush. 'That company of soldiers would have had a few seconds to open fire and kill me, the time it would have taken me to cross the few meters of cleared ground before the bush (on the opposite side of the road to the company). If they missed and I made it to the bush it would be a different story. My chances of escape and success would be a lot greater if I got into that shrubbery'.

At Banda, near Kampala, Museveni disembarked and walked up the hill to Kyambogo Teacher's College. This is where the fearless Valerian Rwaheru resided. Museveni related to Rwaheru what had transpired in Mbale; he also deposited his pistol with him. Later that evening (after a shower and change of clothes), Rwaheru escorted Museveni to Mawingo bus terminal near Nakasero, where Museveni caught a bus for Nairobi. This bus ride was uneventful, at Namanve the vehicle checkpoint had disappeared. Most probably Amin's incompetent soldiers had gone to sleep. Looking out of the window into the darkness as they drove past Namanve, Museveni considered what might have been if the soldier had been more inquisitive earlier that day.

Essentially, Museveni that night retraced the route he had taken earlier that day. This means that he employed the Kampala-Mbale road twice the day after the incident at 49 Maluku Estate, with Amin's thugs still very irritable. This is a remarkable feat and demonstrates that clandestine operations in revolutionary warfare are in effect special operations. A modern day operator would look with envy at Museveni's accomplishments and yet Museveni did this kind of thing all the time, having received no special forces training. A truly remarkable achievement.

After managing to extract herself from the situation that was developing at her house, Beth ran and hid in a cotton field. Today, two schools stand where the cotton field was located in early 1973. These are Maluku Primary School and Hamdan Girls Secondary School. Concealed in the cotton crop she suddenly realised that she had left her two little children in the house. Filled with trepidation and angst, she agonized about the safety of her children. She knew that going back to the house would mean certain death; she could hear military vehicles going back and forth on a road near the field. The whole area seemed to be saturated with soldiers; she learnt later that reinforcements had been ferried from Bugema barracks and brought to the estate. The soldiers surrounded the entire estate and started a vicious search operation. Most of the residents of the estate gripped by fear fled into the bush, where they spent the next couple of days.

There was a young teenager called Sebastino Namirundu. He had just returned from school and was preparing his supper when he heard the commotion outside his home. Peering through a window, he saw numerous soldiers who were in a state of nervous fury. They were rummaging through peoples homes, apparently searching for guerrillas. Namirundu was terrified but did not know what to do; moments went by and finally the petrified youth decided to try and escape. Unfortunately, Namirundu was not successful; Amin's ruffians seized him and accused the poor boy of being a guerrilla. The boy's denials and pleas for mercy were disregarded by Amin's brutal hoodlums. Sebastino Namirundu was publicly executed by Amin's thugs (with another unfortunate individual called Tom Masaba) soon after the Maluku Estate event for absolutely nothing.

This is how Ugandans were savaged by the governments of Milton Obote and Idi Amin, the violence of these regimes knew no bounds, hundreds of thousands of our countrymen and women died in circumstances similar to that poor boy's. It is amazing that today twenty four years after the Okello junta was expelled from power by the forces of the Uganda peoples' revolution, there are revisionists who would seek to obscure this bitter history. These people are apologists of the worst forms of government imaginable, governments that supervised the wholesale slaughter of our compatriots.

Beth's five and three year-old boys had remained in the house when she took flight. William 'Nasa' Mukwana the five year -old and Stanley Pande the three year-old were curious when the commotion started. The elder boy glanced outside and saw the soldiers lifting the bodies of Mwesiga and Kazimoto and placing them in a jeep. He also saw them kicking their neighbour Mrs. Sserunjogi, who for some reason they mistook for Beth. Then he rushed back inside the house and (as infants typically do when looking for a safe place) hid under a bed with his younger brother. From their sanctuary under the bed, they could hear the soldiers rummaging through the house; it is remarkable that the two infants had the discipline and presence of mind to remain concealed. However, soon a soldier lifted the mattress and found the infants. One of the soldiers lifted his rifle and took aim; he was restrained by an elderly soldier who spoke Lugisu. He told his colleague that killing infants was abominable; the soldier who had wanted to shoot the boys relented but argued that these children would grow up to be guerrillas like their parents.

The Mugisu soldier led the children out of the house and escorted them to the house of an uncle of Beth's who lived in the estate. The soldier left the children outside the house and told them to wait for their mother. Fortunately, for little William and Stanley, their aunt, who lived in Busamaga with her family, arrived shortly after this and found the children outside her uncle's house. Their aunt had hurried to check on her relatives when she heard that there had been trouble at Maluku Estate and that many people had been killed by the army.

In the house, the soldiers found the briefcase that Patrick Bukeni had not managed to retrieve before he ran. Inside they found his travellers cheques and identification documents. Bukeni was able to find his way to Kenya where a few days after his arrival a story carried in *The Nation* newspaper said that he had been killed in Mbale. The soldiers also found guns that Maumbe had kept in a water tank (in the house) without Beth's knowledge. The guns found in the house plus the three guns they found in the Volkswagen (which was later towed to Bugema barracks) must have been a windfall achievement for Amin's security machinery. There must have been a lot of congratulatory back slapping going around but they underestimated the strength and resilience of the revolution. No amount of temporary good fortune would save them from the righteous wrath of the Ugandan people.

Beth spent the night in the cotton field horrified at what the fate of her children had been. That night there was a lot of shooting all around her, as the soldiers searched in vain for Museveni. The whole of Mbale town ground to a halt as people fled in terror from the wrath of the soldiers. She could hear shooting coming from the direction of the eucalyptus forest. The next day she spotted a group of people walking on a road that was near the field; she joined them and walked to the estate. There, she went to the house of a lady who was her friend. Her friend lent her a '*busuuti*' dress and headscarf; she changed clothes. Her primary goal was to find out what had happened to her boys and to her great relief that day she learnt that they had not been killed. She spent the next two nights in the toilet of a newly built primary school. 'Those days the toilets were maintained and clean, not like these days', she recalled. On the fourth day she was re-united with her children and then walked with them to Wanale (part of Mt. Elgon), where she took refuge. She also managed to send word to her parents that she was still alive for a rumour had circulated that she had been killed along with her children. Later, her father helped her escape to Kenya where she stayed for sometime posing as a member of the Bukusu people of Kenya (who are close relations of the Bagisu).

Analysis

Let us return to the discussion about Museveni's exhibition of the principle of relative superiority. Clearly when he leapt over the hedge at the house he caught the soldiers completely unawares, in other words he reacted in a manner and at a time that the enemy was unprepared for, i.e. he achieved surprise. Surprise has the effect of mitigating the vulnerability of the agent that attains it. Special operations units strive to gain surprise through a number of means, always seeking to reduce what is called the 'area of vulnerability'. The 'area of vulnerability' is entered into from the moment one starts encountering the enemy's defenses. If you encounter the enemy's defenses early on in an operation then your area of vulnerability is correspondingly greater and the likelihood of mission success diminishes. However, if you run into the enemy defenses late in an operation, then the chances of mission success are greater. The psychological effect that surprise generates is an important tool in the hands of numerically inferior forces.

The action of bounding over the hedge had the effect of temporarily stunning and confusing the soldiers; all of a sudden they were confronted with a situation that they had not anticipated. Museveni's action made what had seemed like a simple and straightforward arrest a much more complicated event, now the soldiers had to exert themselves in chasing after a very fit Museveni. Had Mwesiga and Kazimoto scrammed in different directions at the same time, the sense of chaos generated by this act might have been quite overpowering. Of course, there is no guarantee that all would have escaped, however one can postulate that the chances for success would have been greater.

Special Forces units train operators that when captured by the enemy it is their duty to attempt an escape at the earliest opportunity. The chances for success are greater the earlier one attempts a breakout. The reason the three men did not all attempt to escape is because they had not agreed before being ordered outside on what their response was going to be; in military parlance we call this 'actions on…'. Hence, they had not discussed 'actions on being surrounded by the enemy at Maumbe's house'. They did not have a contingency for this eventuality.

There can be no doubt that once surprise was achieved, Museveni acted with preternatural speed to maintain relative superiority (i.e. the advantage he had attained over Amin's soldiers). Although no one timed the race between Museveni and the Kakwa soldier, we can reasonably be sure that it took seconds for an athletic Museveni to outpace his pursuer. In 1973, Museveni was twenty nine years old; photos from the time reveal a fit young man who was as thin as a rake. His early life as the son of a Muhima pastoralist in the southwest of Uganda, had prepared him for the physical exertions of covert action. As a young boy he would tend his father's cattle for long periods with little or no nourishment. Accustomed to a Spartan existence from his early days, Museveni easily adjusted to the requirements of clandestine operations.

Museveni did not receive any systematic military training until 1975, after the liberation of Mozambique. However, he got sporadic and elementary training from around 1968, and had amassed considerable covert and battlefield experience by 1975.

We know that in 1968-69, Museveni received some minor military training from FRELIMO, in the liberated areas of Northern Mozambique. In Mozambique, he had been introduced to the life of a guerrilla movement in the throes of violent conflict. On that occasion, Museveni and seven other students, all members of the University Students African Revolutionary Front (USARF), a radical student organization formed at the University of Dar-es-Salaam in 1967, had experienced some strafing by Portuguese ground attack aircraft. Later on, in 1969 Museveni received some rudimentary weapons training in North Korea, learning how to operate a Kalashnikov and a pistol.

As was mentioned earlier, in September 1972, Museveni was in the thick of the fighting from the Tanzanian border to Mbarara. It was in that botched effort that Museveni first fired a shot in anger, at Kabereebere; Museveni led a platoon of rebel fighters in unleashing a torrent of gunfire at an enemy troop carrier. Moments later, Museveni and two others approached the lorry in a leopard crawl, to find that its occupants had scampered leaving a treasure trove of guns in the vehicle. Later that same day, Museveni opened fire on an enemy jeep near Agip Motel in Mbarara, dispersing the occupants. Still later, as the attackers approached Mbarara barracks, Museveni had shot a very large man leading a group of around six soldiers near the main gate. The enemy soldiers approached as if to surrender, with their weapons held aloft. Museveni ordered them to drop their weapons, the men kept advancing with their weapons. Museveni opened up and hit the large man. The man along with the rest of the soldiers ran and took cover behind an anthill. Museveni and his comrades kept firing in the direction of the anthill. One man called Angetta, started lobbing grenades behind the anthill. In the fighting throughout that day and in the subsequent withdrawal back to Tanzania, Museveni was to demonstrate his trademark courage, resolve, presence of mind and an uncanny sixth sense for danger. Like Erwin Rommel's famous sense of 'Fingerspitzengefühl', i.e. his ability to second guess the enemy, Museveni in Mbarara demonstrated an ability to assess situations and extract immediate and relevant decisions.

After two attempts at assaulting the barracks in Mbarara had disintegrated, Museveni started questioning the wisdom of continuing the attack. In his autobiography he writes, 'After assessing the situation, I advised the two groups to withdraw to Nyamityobora forest... We stayed in the forest until 2.00 pm., resting and reflecting on our losses, while Amin's soldiers randomly lobbed shells at us with light mortars... After we had rested a while, I advised that we should cut our losses and go back to Tanzania. It took some time to convince the remnants of our force to withdraw in an orderly fashion. They were still drunk on the lies of their leaders who had been telling them that there was a substantial fifth column waiting inside Uganda to assist them take over power as soon as a few shots were fired at the border. They had been led to believe that this would be an easy war'[16]. After much argument, Museveni was able to persuade forty six men to withdraw under his leadership back to Tanzania. In any event, he was responsible for saving the lives of those men; for out of 330 men that crossed into Uganda (on the Mbarara axis) earlier that day, only Museveni's 46 lived to talk about it. Unfortunately, for Museveni's close friends and comrades like Mwesigwa Black, Raiti Omongin and Kahunga Bagira were not among those that got away.

Therefore, there can be little doubt that by 1973 Museveni was familiar with the nature of war. He would have readily accepted Clausewitz's description of war being the realm of [*danger, physical exertion, uncertainty and chance*]¹⁷ having experienced this first hand. Although familiarity with the environment of war does not in itself enhance relative superiority, it certainly prepares the individual for the vicissitudes that all warfare embraces. Lieutenant Theodor Werner a contemporary of Erwin Rommel in the Wuertemberg Mountain Battalion in World War I had this to say about this incomparable warrior:

> 'Anybody who once came under the spell of his personality turned into a real soldier. However tough the strain he seemed inexhaustible. He seemed to know just what the enemy was like and how they would probably react. His plans were often startling, instinctive, obscure. He had an exceptional imagination, and it enabled him to hit on the most unexpected solutions to tough situations. When there was danger, he was always out in front, calling on us to follow. He seemed to know no fear whatever. His men idolized him and had boundless faith in him'[18].

Such extraordinary gifts of mind and temperament (every bit the measure of genius) were (in Rommel's case) constantly honed in the deadly milieu of war. It is said that although Rommel detested war as an insane business, he relished it when there was no alternative. He fully immersed himself in it when it was thrust upon him, always leading from the front impervious to any personal risks. It was this reveling in war that gave him virtuosity in its practice, just like an athlete who trains relentlessly improves his performance. In similar fashion, Museveni who selflessly threw himself into the hazards of violent revolution achieved matchless talent in this enterprise.

What could have been done differently? We broached this subject earlier in the chapter. By having no contingencies, no 'actions on' the three men exposed the (as yet) undeveloped nature of their knowledge of troop leading procedures (TLPs) and the orders process. Whether a unit is going on reconnaissance, a fighting patrol, to set an ambush or for a raid there must always be contingency planning. The army has codified this in its formal orders; contingencies or 'actions on' are enshrined under paragraph 3a. Execution, Concept of Operations and specifically under Scheme of Maneuver. When a commander reaches this stage in reading his orders, he must tell his subordinates what will happen in case of unexpected changes, for example, if it's a patrol going to set an ambush, the patrol leader must go through actions on contact prior to the objective, actions on getting lost, actions on obstacles, actions on the ambush site being compromised, actions on the objective itself, etc.

A professional army should have all this information readily available for tactical commanders in the form of tactical aide memoires (TAMS), so that commanders do not omit important steps. Once a commander is done with all the 5 paragraphs of a formal order, i.e. from paragraph 1 (Situation) to paragraph 5 (Command and Signal), then his subordinates must disseminate this information to their own men and when all this is done, all have to rehearse everything that was communicated in the orders. 'Attention to detail' is the creed that all decent military organizations live by; sloppiness means mission failure and worse.

In his autobiography, Museveni admits that up to this point (i.e. the incident at Maluku Estate) their little band of revolutionaries had operated in a collegial manner. There was no clear chain of command, decisions were reached after consultation and as much as possible consensus was sought. The loss of his close friends taught Museveni to disregard any attempts at being civil when it came to clandestine/military operations. From then on his approach to all matters military was direct and categorical.

Therefore, what could have been done differently at 49 Maluku Estate? Had the three men agreed (or had one of them ordered the rest) that in the event they encountered soldiers they were to fight, this would have prepared all of them (mentally) for this possibility. There would have been no contemplation of contrary positions. All would have acted in unison in accordance with the order they had received. If in addition to the guidance to fight, there had been some arrangement for rendezvousing in the event that they were separated, this would have been very helpful.

Clearly, the men erred by not leaving a sentry outside. A sentry posted outside would have alerted the rest (inside the house) of the approaching soldiers; ideally, this alarm should have been by way of the sentry opening fire on the lead soldiers. This would have inflicted casualties, caused confusion, slowed them down and consequently bought time for the men to make their escape to a pre-arranged rendezvous point. Che Guevara cautioned nascent guerrilla movements against making the mistake of sleeping in houses (even the houses of supporters) because of the limited 'arcs of fire' that enclosed spaces present. Better to sleep in a garden or backyard near the house, he advised. Similarly, in special operations dropping sentries outside when you enter a building is absolutely vital.

The use of great volumes of firepower always throws an opponent. If the weight of firepower employed by the men had been great then their chances of success might have been enhanced. Indeed, firepower is one way of achieving surprise either by the weight of firepower or the type of firepower. For this reason the use of explosives is particularly helpful, grenades can kill and maim people within a fifteen meter radius. Had the men hurled a couple of these into the advancing soldiers, it would have completely disorganized them and killed quite a few as well.

Conclusion

Let it be remembered that the reason for this clandestine activity in the first place, was the attempt by Museveni and his associates to ignite the fires of a guerrilla struggle against Idi Amin's dictatorship. By the time of the incident at Maluku Estate, these exertions were not going well at all. Almost every guerrilla group that was inaugurated by the revolutionaries was instantaneously detected by the junta. This was the reason for the visit to Mbale by the three men that day. They had come to check on the guerrilla fighters that had been relocated from Bunya forest in Busoga and were supposed to be at Maumbe's farm house in Busiu. Their presence in Bunya forest had been compromised by certain ill-disciplined elements amongst them. Once they got to the house in Busiu, they found that Maumbe had moved them out of fear for their security, since word of their presence had gotten out to the local community. The discipline of these early guerrilla groups left a lot to be desired and it was not until the Montepuez group (that was trained in Mozambique for 2 years under the personal command of Museveni from 1975-77) that finally a faction emerged that had the requisite discipline for the prosecution of a resistance war based on Mao Zedong's people's war strategy.

Events were to conspire to delay the implementation of a people's war in Uganda for a further four years (from 1977-1981), but not to save Amin's hide. On October 30th 1978, Amin made the colossal mistake of invading the Kagera Salient in Tanzania. An enraged President Julius Nyerere declared that by invading Tanzania, Amin had given them the cause (*sabaabu*) to fight him, they already had the will (*nia*) and the means (*uwezo*) to do so. In six months, the Tanzanian People's Defense Forces (TPDF) reinforced by elements of Museveni's Front for National Salvation (FRONASA)* and Obote's Kikosi Maalum (Special Battalion or Unit) hurled the dictator from power.

This conventional conflict saw the intervention of Arab forces i.e. Libya and the Palestinian Liberation Organization (PLO) on the side of the dictator. They attempted to salvage Amin's crumbling regime. The Arabs suffered severe losses at the hands of the TPDF juggernaut, with over 300 killed by the termination of hostilities. On the 11th of April 1979 the heroic *wakombozi* (liberators) took Kampala and ended that war. Unknown to the victorious liberators in 1979, this war and its political aftermath would necessitate the start of the resistance war.

We now turn our attention to events after the fall of Amin and the battles that defined the Ugandan resistance war.

---

*   FRONASA was an anti-Amin dissident group, that was formed in the early 1970s by Yoweri Museveni. It was based in Tanzania

Notes

11. William H. McRaven, Spec Ops: *Case Studies in Special Operations Warfare Theory and Practice*, (The Random House Publishing Group, New York, 1996), 4

12. Carl Von Clausewitz, *On War*, Edited and Translated by Michael Howard and Peter Paret, (New York, Princeton University Press, 1993), 130.

13. Carl Von Clausewitz, *On War*, Edited and Translated by Michael Howard and Peter Paret, (New York, Princeton University Press, 1993), 115.

14. Carl Von Clausewitz, *On War*, (New York, Princeton University Press, 1993), 115.

15. Yoweri Kaguta Museveni, *Sowing The Mustard Seed*, The Struggle for Freedom and Democracy in Uganda, (Malaysia, Macmillan Publishers Limited, 2007), 80.

16. Yoweri Kaguta Museveni, *Sowing The Mustard Seed*, (Malaysia, Macmillan Publishers Limited, 2007), 67-68.

17. Carl Von Clausewitz, *On War*, (New York, Princeton University Press, 1993), 116-117.

18. Erwin Rommel and an example of Heideggerian Authenticity, by Michael Capistran, http://www.raleightavern.org/rommel.htm accessed September 24, 2008

3

To Start a War

'Every man thinks meanly of himself for not having been a soldier'
Samuel Johnson

Clausewitz counseled that 'no one starts a war- or rather, no one in his senses ought to do so – without first being clear in his mind what he intends to achieve by that war and how he intends to conduct it'[19]. Practitioners of violent revolution have offered a number of explanations for what factors motivate individuals (ordinarily engaged in peaceable pursuits) to resort to violent struggle. Che Guevara famously posited that there were 'objective' and 'subjective' conditions that were responsible for this transformation in people's attitudes. Che explained that 'objective' conditions were the realities of a given political or social situation, the hard undeniable truths of exploitation, oppression and injustice. 'Subjective' conditions had to do with human factors, e.g. the realization by a population that violent revolution was the only solution (i.e. the level of 'revolutionary consciousness'), also, the dynamism of the revolutionary party and the eloquence of its leadership. Naturally, by discussing objective and subjective conditions Che kept faith with the Marxist tradition.

Marx had postulated that 'force is the midwife of every old society pregnant with a new one'[20]. This was consistent with his idea about the innate materialist contradictions in all societies that propel history – later to be described by Frederick Engels as 'dialectical materialism'. Marx perceived historical movements as a product of certain tensions that exist in every society between those who controlled the factors of production (land and capital) and those who worked for them. This friction, or clash, between the classes produced new historical realities and hence new societies. Che's contention that revolution was probable once certain objective and subjective conditions had been attained was a natural progression of this Marxist argument.

Central to this perception of human events is the notion that certain laws govern the progress of history. From these concepts it is clear that there is a determinism about Marxism, a certain denial of the idea that human beings are free agents having free will, which often does not find resonance in reality. The individual is many times critical to the development of human events. For instance, what would have become of the Chinese revolution without the iron will of a Mao? Or the Cuban revolution without the audacity of a Fidel or Che? There can be little doubt that the Ugandan revolution without the courage and faith of Yoweri Museveni would be a very difficult if not impossible enterprise.

It is this ambiguity about the role of individuals (some of whom are exceptionally important to the success of revolutionary movements) in the making of history that presents the greatest problem with the deterministic notions inherent in Marxism's conception of history. The fatalism exhibited by slogans such as 'the individual is dispensable' only serves to expose the error in this school of thought. We can say with certainty, that sometimes in the history of societies there arise exceptional individuals who are absolutely indispensable for the advancement of their people's cause.

In the case of the Ugandan resistance war, some in the leadership of the rebel army had more profitable (and safer) opportunities they could have pursued. They had 'options' in the words of General Elly Tumwine (the leading commander of the National Resistance Army for most of the bush war). General Tumwine (now a four star retired general) had trained as a teacher prior to the war. He recalled the important role Museveni played in educating and enlightening them before the war. In his words, 'At the core of the NRA's brilliant military strategy, was the amount of time the leadership took in mentally preparing and educating us'. For General Tumwine, mental preparation of the individual, in terms of sharpening his/her convictions and demonstrating that victory is possible (notwithstanding the hardships of struggle), is much more important than the amount of arms one has access to initially. It is people who win wars not weaponry.

This position is strikingly similar to Mao Zedong's assertion that, 'Weapons are an important factor in war, but not the decisive factor; it is people, not things that are decisive. The contest of strength is not only a contest of military and economic power, but also a contest of human power and morale'[21]. Present day U.S. Army thinking echoes Mao's teaching when it declares 'people [are] the army's most important asset'[22], in the words of General John M. Keane, Vice Chief of Staff for the United States Army (2001).

For General Tumwine, this indoctrination started in 1979 during the Tanzanian led anti-Amin war. He joined the struggle out of a desire to do anything to get rid of the dictator. 'I wanted to serve in whatever capacity, whether as a cook or soldier', he recalled. He joined Museveni's FRONASA because he knew the man from an earlier interaction. Museveni was his teacher in primary six (at the time Museveni was in his senior six vacation, prior to leaving for Dar es Salaam University). Elly Tumwine was enlisted at Ngarama in Isingiro district in early 1979 and it quickly became clear that he had joined a serious bunch of people. The recruits were introduced to intense political indoctrination (called *'siasa'* in Kiswahili). By his own admission he had never thought of 'a revolution' up to that point in time. However, very soon he was fully immersed in it. They would study the history of Uganda's armies, from the colonial Kings African Rifles (KAR) to Amin's, which they were in the process of dismembering. Additionally, they would study at length the anti-colonial liberation movements of Africa. 'We used to say to ourselves… my God what a colossal task we have in saving our country.' This indoctrination served two purposes; one was to show the recruits the immensity of the task that awaited them; the second was to rally and energize them. 'We felt that we could rescue our homeland', General Tumwine recollected when the author interviewed him.

This preparation of dedicated cadres had begun in late 1976, when Yoweri Museveni recruited 28 young men to act as the nucleus of the Ugandan revolutionary movement – then based in Tanzania. After the disasters and false starts of 1972 and 1973, it seems Museveni had come to the same realization as had another exponent of violent revolution 74 years before him. In 1902, the Russian revolutionary Vladimir Illych Ulyanov (Lenin) wrote *'What Is To Be Done?'* In this pamphlet, he made a number of important observations about the condition of the proletarian revolution at that time and its prospects for success. He concluded that some of Marx's assumptions about capitalism (made in the middle of the 19th Century) had not been borne out by real events. The welfare of workers had improved (not degenerated as Marx had hypothesized) aided by the activism of trade-unions. The workers' appetite for violent struggle had correspondingly reduced.

Lenin surmised that the proletariat on its own was incapable of attaining to the revolutionary consciousness necessary for a complete overthrow of the bourgeois state. He asserted that the 'history of all countries bears out the fact that through their own powers alone, the working class can develop only a trade-union consciousness'[23]. What was required was a body of committed activists for the proletarian revolution, 'professional' revolutionaries you could say, who would dedicate themselves wholly to educating the proletariat and preparing them for the revolution. He called this body of committed revolutionaries 'the vanguard party' of the proletariat. Hounded and persecuted by Tsarist Russia's secret police, Lenin naturally argued that this revolutionary vanguard must utilize clandestine methods in order to survive.

In similar vein, Museveni had come to the realization by 1976 that only a body of dedicated revolutionaries, could spark the fires of resistance in Uganda. This vanguard would undergo military training in Montepuez in Mozambique. In the training in Mozambique, Museveni started organizing the underpinnings of the ideology of the Ugandan resistance. These ideological tenets included a rejection of tribalism, a refusal of adventurism (of both the political and military kind), the embracing of pan-Africanism and a strong (even severe) emphasis on martial discipline. From amongst the ranks of the Montepuez cadre emerged two of the most important commanders of the resistance war, i.e. General Salim Saleh Rufu (whose real name was Caleb Akandwanaho) and Major General Fred Rwigema (RIP). Other important figures from

Montepuez include Lt. General Ivan Koreta (presently the deputy Chief of Defense Forces of the UPDF) and the late Brigadier Chefe Ali.

The practice of embracing Arabic or Muslim pseudonyms by some of the revolutionaries started at this time and served two purposes. First it identified the bearer as a member of the religion of Islam (although neither 'Salim Saleh'or 'Chefe Ali' was a Muslim) and thus guaranteed that they would not raise the suspicions of the Ugandan authorities (who were then pre-dominantly drawn from Amin's Kakwa tribesmen, many of whom are Muslims). For this reason Amin's regime was generally perceived as pro-Islam. Secondly (and most importantly), pseudonyms ensured that one's relatives back home were not targeted by the authorities, since it would not be easy to link a troublesome guerrilla to a particular family.

'The core or nucleus is the strength of an organization', General Tumwine remarked 'and I can assure you our core (comprised of the Montepuez group, the Monduli trained officers and the Cuban trained intelligence operatives) was very, very strong!' 'Under the ideological guidance of our leader Yoweri Museveni we all knew and had been prepared for a long people's war by February 6th 1981', General Tumwine observed.

The ideological principles of the nascent Ugandan resistance movement were linked to the anti-colonial and anti-imperialist stance of the liberation struggles, then raging across Africa. Museveni's own ideological proximity to Julius Nyerere of Tanzania and Samora Machel of Mozambique ensured that the Ugandan resistance movement would follow in the path of the African liberation struggles. 'How could we have been anything different?' General Tumwine commented, 'The Montepuez group was there training in Mozambique, Frente de Libertação de Moçambique (or FRELIMO) were our brothers in the struggle'. 'In the African context, a revolutionary or freedom fighter must be a pan-Africanist, the two go together' the General told me thoughtfully. 'The only difference was that we were not going to be fighting Portuguese or British colonialists', he continued, 'We were going to fight the rump colonial state, which had African politicians and African soldiers but did not serve the interests of the people. It was an anti-people establishment, a quisling regime, serving the interests of others'. 'This was the great innovation in the Ugandan situation, this was our value-addition to revolutionary warfare and liberation struggles in Africa', General Tumwine mused.

Notwithstanding the ideological intimacy between the nascent Ugandan resistance movement in the late 1970s and liberation movements like FRELIMO and Tanzania's Chama Cha Mapinduzi (or Revolutionary Party), which were both socialist inclined, Museveni made it clear from the start that he and his associates were not communists. 'Our leader used to tell us from the beginning that we will not fall into the trap of being labeled pro-east or pro-west', General Tumwine recalled, 'We were always pro-ourselves, pro-Uganda'. An intense nationalism is at the core of the ideology of the Ugandan resistance.

Two elements were at the root of the NRA's successes as a guerrilla army, one was this rigorous ideological preparation of cadres and the second aspect was an almost religious adherence to the idea that 'the people are supreme'. If any action appeared to threaten the NRA's relationship with the '*wanainchi*' (the people), it was immediately torpedoed. In every engagement, every skirmish, every operation, due consideration was given to this principle and those who fell afoul of it were instantaneously and very publicly disciplined. These two ideas were at the heart of the NRA's strength from its inception until about the time of the third attack on Kabamba in early 1985. After the third (and successful) battle of Kabamba, it became increasingly clear that the NRA's strength was becoming irresistible, recruits started flocking to what seemed to be the winning side of a very brutal civil war.

However, at the beginning not even the most fervent supporter could have given the tiny rebel army much of a chance. The odds were stacked against Museveni and his comrades to say the least. At the time in Uganda, outside of Museveni and his small coterie of revolutionaries, no one had an inkling of what 'people's war' actually meant or what it entailed. Museveni's anti-Amin activities during the 1970s and his prominent role in the Tanzanian-led war to topple the dictator, had bestowed a certain reputation for derring-do upon the young revolutionary leader. So when the war started in February of 1981 (as Museveni had promised it would in the event of rigged general elections), people were not necessarily surprised. After all, this was the kind of audacious action that Museveni was famous for, but whether it would work or not, was a different question. The overwhelming majority were inclined to think the latter.

To be able to harness people's convictions is the pinnacle of leadership and of organizational skill. Just like the early Christians, who driven by the gospel of Jesus Christ, were ready to die facing down the power of imperial Rome eventually overcame all hardships, Museveni and his vanguard knew that the power of human convictions can overcome mountains. The essential pre-condition in these circumstances is effective and inspirational leadership that is able to articulate and demonstrate that victory is possible, even inevitable. In the early days of the NRA, all military operations were fashioned to amplify one idea – we can win!

Notes

19. Carl Von Clausewitz, *On War*, (New York, Princeton University Press, 1993), 700.
20. Thinkexist.com, Karl Marx Quotes, http://thinkexist.com/quotation/force_is_the_midwife_of_every_old_society/180973.html accessed January 25, 2009.
21. Quotations from Mao Tse Tung, http://www.marxists.org/reference/archive/mao/works/red-book/ch12.htm accessed January 28, 2009.
22. Prepared Statement of General John M. Keane, Vice Chief of Staff, United States Army, http://www.globalsecurity.org/military/library/congress/2001_hr/01-06-26keane.htm accessed January 28, 2009.
23. Soviet Democracy, Wikipedia, http://en.wikipedia.org/wiki/Soviet_democracy, accessed February 7, 2009.

Picture Section A

Shaka Zulu

Maumbe's house in Maluku Estate in Mbale. Inset: A recent picture of Maumbe Mukwana

Museveni as a student in Dar es Salaam Universty Tanzania

Mwesiga Martin

58 *Battles of the Ugandan Resistance: A Tradition of Maneuver*

Presidents Julius Nyerere of Tanzania and Samora Machel of Mozambique

FRONASA fighters: Fred Rubereza and Gen. Ivan Koreta

Sebastino Namirundu and Tom Masaba shortly before they were executed by Amin's soldiers

Bodies of Ugandan dissidents killed in the 1972 invasion

Tanzanian soldiers fighting to overthrow Idi Amin in 1979

Top military leaders of UNLA in 1979:
Omaria, Museveni and Ojok at Army Headquarters

4

The Clarion Call: First Battle of Kabamba

> 'I began the revolution with 82 men. If I had to do it again, I would do it with 10 or 15 and absolute faith. It does not matter how small you are if you have faith and a plan of action.'
> Fidel Castro

As part of measures to create a national army (the Uganda National Liberation Army) after the ouster of Idi Amin Dada in 1979, FRONASA units (organized in 'columns') and Milton Obote's 'Kikosi Maalum' (or Special Battalion) had started re-organizing and re-training at Kabamba, Mubende, Nakasongola and Masindi. There were problems from the start, with FRONASA fighters feeling that recruitment into the new national army was skewed and they were intentionally being targeted for de-mobilization. There was a lot of truth in these sentiments: the Chief of Staff of the new army, Oyite Ojok, was an Obote loyalist and he was determined to weed out FRONASA elements from the new national army through the recruitment process. A number of justifications were used to exclude FRONASA cadres; these included nationality, medical condition and physical attributes. The issue of nationality was meant to target FRONASA members of Rwandese

Tutsi extraction. Many of these like Fred Rwigema had been exiled at a very early age and knew their adopted country (Uganda) more than they knew their own homeland. Fred Rwigema had fought as a liberator (*mukombozi*) along with other FRONASA militants to free the country from the grip of Amin's insanity; now he was being reimbursed with xenophobia and paranoia on the part of Ojok and his gang.

The only valid grounds for de-mobilization was the health of applicants; however, given the collapse in the health care system in the country, it is questionable whether the army recruiters had the facilities to make a true and accurate assessment of an individual's health. The most ridiculous parameter for de-mobilizing a soldier was that he was not 'tall enough'. It seems the Kikosi Maalum crowd had inherited this notion from the British colonial army. The Kings African Rifles (KAR) recruited most of their manpower from certain tribes that according to the colonialists exhibited 'martial' characteristics. In Uganda, these were mostly the northern tribes, some of which have tall people. Needless to say, these notions were linked in some way with the completely flawed ideas of racial aptitude, i.e. certain groups are more gifted in certain activities than others. In the same way, the Bahima and Batutsi of Uganda, Rwanda and Burundi were identified as innate leaders and in some way connected to Europeans. Naturally, all this claptrap has been put where it belongs, on history's dung heap of bad ideas. However, in the case of Uganda, Rwanda and Burundi not before a tremendous amount of blood was spilled. Of course, the circumstances in all three countries were quite different.

The idea that tall individuals are somehow better suited to military service is fantastic, of course; you can have a tall person whose fitness and willpower are ideal for the military profession; but the same is true of a short person. With regards to physical attributes, the only way of identifying individuals who will make good soldiers is through rigorous training. It is arduous training that tests the fitness and mental qualities of a soldier in the making. I have seen superb soldiers who just happened to be short and quite pathetic soldiers who happened to be tall and the reverse is true. These days no professional soldier worthy of the name would make such ridiculous statements and British colleagues blush in embarrassment when told about the recruiting parameters of the KAR.

However, for Oyite Ojok and the recruiters of the UNLA this was the law of Moses, there was no deviating from it. Stories are told of how the recruiters (invariably Kikosi Maalum) would whack the measuring ruler on the scalps of some FRONASA recruits who were clearly tall enough to qualify. The pain of the blow would make the recruits cringe and the recruiters would then declare them to be below the mark.

The decommissioning of arms was part of this effort at building a national army. FRONASA fighters were compelled to disarm, in order to be re-issued with new registered arms once the re-organization was over. This caused huge consternation amongst FRONASA ranks, resistance to the proposed disarmament grew. It took the personal intervention of Yoweri Museveni to keep things from spiraling out of control. He explained the situation to the FRONASA men and women, then supervised the disarmament process. Some elements refused outright to be disarmed; notable amongst these was Fred Nkuranga (who took the nom de guerre of 'Fred Rubereza'). Fred Rubereza (RIP) was a prince of the south-western kingdom of Ankole, the son of Omugabe (King) Gasyonga. He had made a name for himself in the Tanzanian-led anti-Amin war. He was a dashing, fearless and unpredictable character. His FRONASA colleagues both loved and feared him, not least because of his considerable martial arts skills, which he was not averse to practicing on the unfortunate souls that provoked him. He claimed that his rifle was a personal possession and that, therefore, he would not hand it over.

These guns were collected and stored at different installations, one of which was the armory at Kabamba Training School. In the opinion of General Tumwine, the attack on Kabamba served three purposes. First of all, it was a call to action, a clarion call for the whole Ugandan nation. It fulfilled Museveni's promise that he would launch a 'bush war' if the 1980 general elections were rigged by Milton Obote's Uganda Peoples' Congress. It also served as the signal for FRONASA cadres dispersed throughout the country (and army) that a new liberation war had commenced. Thirdly, in General Tumwine's words, 'We were going back to reclaim our guns; we knew they were there and we wanted them back'.

Once the decision to mount an armed insurrection against the UPC establishment was taken, Museveni worked with a small group of FRONASA cadres on the preparations for war. Most of them had participated in the Tanzanian-led anti-Amin war and were now junior officers in the UNLA.

The first battle of Kabamba was preceded by a period of reconnoitering that established the strength of the Tanzanian garrison force there, the number of recruits being trained and crucially the routine of the installation. This information was provided by FRONASA agents stationed at the training school at the time, i.e. the late Sergeant Kato Patrick and the late Brigadier Tadeo Kanyankore. From this accurate intelligence picture, the plotters were able to determine the most opportune moment to attack. It would have to be in the early morning hours and not at dawn as military custom dictates. At dawn the garrison force (comprised of 'several companies of Tanzanian soldiers'[24]) would be in their stand-to positions (and hence would be alert). However, once stand-to was over around about 8.00 am, there was a marked drop in vigilance. The bulk of the garrison force would disperse into the interior of the camp to conduct training, lounge in their accommodation and carry out other administrative tasks. Only a small force would remain to provide security at the front gate and armory.

Furthermore, this reconnaissance was able to ascertain the distance between the front gate and the armory, which was of huge importance to the men who were preparing to become guerrillas. Given the small numbers* of the attackers, it was crucial that the armory be as close as possible to the entrance of the camp, since they could not hope to sustain a deep penetration of a large military camp. The armory at Kabamba was approximately 100 meters from the front gate, which could be covered rapidly by the attackers, allowing for a rapid and surreptitious seizure of this objective.

Museveni and his men hoped to capitalize on the fact that no one knew there was a war on, the element of surprise would aid the attack on Kabamba. Achieving surprise (with all the psychological benefits associated with it) would be crucial in this battle.

At 5.30 pm on the 5th of February 1981, 34 men (of whom only 27 were armed) boarded a lorry driven by Andrew Lutaya (now a retired Brigadier) and left Kampala. Hours later Museveni

---

* Essentially, the attacking force at the first battle of Kabamba was comprised of Museveni's escorts and the few FRONASA cadres that were in the Kampala area in the weeks preceding the commencement of the war.

in the company of Sam Magara (RIP) and Charles Tusiime (who was driving) followed in a pick-up. The plan required the force to assemble at a point about 3 km from Makoole trading center (although in 1981 there wasn't much there) on the Sembabule-Mubende road.

The location had the unique marker of a burnt out hull of an armored reconnaissance vehicle, a remnant of the anti-Amin war. Once the lorry got to this point, it stopped according to the plan and the men disembarked. They entered the bush and started changing into uniforms. They also checked their weapons and those that had rifles cocked them. Code-words for the operation were issued at this location. Lieutenant Elly Tumwine was in charge of this battle preparation.

At around 3.00 am, Museveni and Magara arrived in a Peugeot 304 and took charge. Museveni had no time to relate to his comrades that the pick-up and some poor planning on the part of his driver had almost succeeded in making him miss the start of the war. The pick-up with which they had started their journey in Kampala had gotten a flat tyre at Katigondo about 19 kilometers from Masaka on the Nyendo-Sembabule road. It was then that their driver announced that he had not brought a spare tyre. Museveni had to walk back to Nyendo (19 kilometers to the rear) in the dead of night to the home of Nathan Ruyondo and sell him some story about needing to borrow his Peugeot 304 to go and attend a relative's wedding. Needless to say, Ruyondo never saw his car again; it had been requisitioned for the prosecution of the war.

Museveni organized the force into three sections. The first section would be led by Sam Magara and would attack the armory, the second under Elly Tumwine would dispose of the sentries at the front gate and the third under Hannington Mugabi would make for the quartermaster stores. There was also a force comprised of around four individuals that included Paul Kagame (now President of Rwanda) that was armed with pistols and was supposed to attack the camp's communication room. The sections were briefed on their targets and on the concept of operations. The men then climbed into their transports and drove until they got close to Nkonge (near the railway line) before halting again.

However, in the darkness somehow the young Tumwine had been separated from his comrades. He emerged from the bush only to see the tail lights of the small convoy in the distance. He had no choice but to run after the two vehicles. With his back pack on, he was still able to cover the distance in a very short time. He finally caught up with the lorry at around 4.30 am (at Nkonge); it had parked at the side of the dirt road. The Peugeot had been sent forward to do some last minute reconnaissance of the target. Lieutenant Tumwine (breathing heavily from the run) rapped on the passenger door of the lorry and Museveni peered out. He asked him what he was doing? Tumwine related how he had been left behind and had to run to catch up. Museveni then disembarked and allowed Tumwine to sit in the front passenger seat. He went to sit in the rear with the rest (this was to prevent raising the curiosity of the sentries at Kabamba, in the event they saw and recognized Museveni). The attackers waited out the remaining few hours before H-hr in this location, many grabbed a few hours of sleep.

At around 8.25 am on Friday the 6th of February, the two vehicles approached the front gate of Kabamba Training School. The lorry was in the lead, with the Peugeot carrying Sam Magara and some members of his section following. A little distance before they got to the front gate, the lorry stopped and the group of around four men armed with pistols (that was meant to attack the communications room) disembarked. This was near the officers' quarters. Once the lorry got to the front gate, Lieutenant Tumwine disembarked from the front passenger seat; as he did so, some members of his section started disembarking from the rear of the lorry. He approached the two sentries who were there. One sentry (a corporal) had his rifle and the other one (a private) did not. The suspicions of the sentries were right away aroused by the large number of soldiers that took positions behind him with their weapons at the ready. Tumwine started to engage them in conversation by telling them he had brought supplies for the camp from General Headquarters. As he spoke, the sentries could see more soldiers disembarking from the rear of the lorry and beginning to take positions behind the lorry (this was mainly Hannington Mugabi's section).

With their suspicions aroused, the private who had left his gun in a small guard room (co-located with the front gate) went back to retrieve it. Then the Peugeot (whose engine had been revving all this time) shot past the lorry and raced towards the armory. That was it for the sentries. They opened the safes of their Kalashnikovs and Tumwine shouted the codeword for open fire, '*chakula*' (food). Tumwine opened the safe of his rifle and shot the corporal who was now trying to aim his rifle at him. The rest of his section opened fire and shot the private. The two men did not keel over and die immediately but ran and crawled in the direction of some tin huts that were adjacent to the front gate. They were pursued by Tumwine and his section. Both sentries were dispatched before they got far. Once the group composed of around four men that were armed with pistols heard the shots at the front gate, they assumed the attack had commenced and opened fire as well. They were still behind the officers' quarters.

The firing at the front gate had rallied the Tanzanian sentry of the armory, who took charge of some machineguns and prepared to repulse any attack on the armory. The armory at Kabamba was an underground structure, composed of strong concrete. Any assailant would have to approach it in one of two ways; either directly via a large and open concrete walkway (that sloped towards the entrance), or by way of a rocky overhang above the entrance to the armory. On this occasion, the attackers attempted to approach the armory directly via the concrete walkway. However, with the vigilant Tanzanian sentry, it quickly became clear that this was impossible. Essentially, the sentry had a clear field of fire and would have used it to devastating effect on anyone trying to assault by way of the walkway. All attempts by Magara and his section to assault the armory were quickly snuffed out by the sustained fire of the sentry's machineguns.

Hannington Mugabi and his section had raced from the front gate once the shooting started; they proceeded towards the quartermaster stores. As they ran, one of them Suicide Katungi (RIP) started firing shots from his G-3 into the air. He held it in one hand and fired as he ran. At the stores they were met by Kyakabale and Sgt. Kato who were waiting to join them there. Tadeo Kanyankore (another rebel collaborator), was also present at the training school but did not join them until about eight months later.

Museveni positioned himself on a small mound near the front gate and watched the attack on the armory. There was generalized shooting throughout the camp by now, fire started being directed towards the front gate and mound where Museveni stood, it came from the direction of the staff quarters. Tumwine and his section took cover and anxiously looked over to Museveni who was still standing erect on the mound. Tumwine implored him to take cover but he refused. Then Magara returned to the front gate from the attempt to assault the armory. He and some of his men were in the Peugeot 304. He reported that the attack on the armory had been foiled by the sentry's stubborn resistance. Undeterred, Museveni ordered Tumwine and Magara to join forces and attack the armory again. The two men led their sections in a renewed attack on the armory. They shook out into an extended line and advanced on the armory. As they approached the armory the volume of fire from within increased. The attackers took cover as bullets zipped past them. Akanga Byaruhanga (RIP) crawled forward and lobbed a grenade in, it did not explode. Then they fired their only anti-tank rifle grenade but it had little effect. The tenacious sentry could not be dislodged. Both Tumwine and Magara started getting concerned that the attack was taking too long and that the enemy might organize a counter-attack at any moment. Finally, resolving that the first duty of a guerrilla is to survive, the men in the two sections decided there was no point in pressing the attack any further.

Magara's and Tumwine's sections returned to the front gate where they urged Museveni to order a withdrawal. Museveni ordered that guns be collected from the places in the camp which the attackers had succeeded in capturing, i.e. the communications center, the military transport section and guardroom. A total of eight vehicles were captured and with these, the attackers withdrew. They drove from Kabamba in the direction of Nabingola. The attack had lasted about one hour and the force had sustained only one significant casualty, Julius Chihandae (now a retired Colonel) who was shot through the leg.

Analysis

The first battle of Kabamba has earned a reputation for having been somewhat of a botched job. Evidently, the main object of the attack was never realized (the seizure of arms from the armory); however, there is a lot to be said for the notion that it was a qualified success. There were a lot of positives in the battle and in the preparations before the battle. The intelligence obtained in the weeks and months prior to the 6th of February was first rate; it allowed the plotters to know the most propitious moment to strike. Furthermore, the intelligence enabled an understanding of the routine of the facility and the dispositions of troops at different times of the day.

Once the target had been selected, those in the know must be credited for having kept their mouths shut. In other words, operational security (OPSEC) was rigorously applied. There is no indication that the garrison at Kabamba had been alerted of the imminent attack; had they been, then there is no doubt that the attackers would have suffered horrendous losses. Attacking an armed garrison is not the favored technique of insurgents' intent on launching a 'protracted' war. This is because often armed garrisons have entrenched positions and clear fields of fire. Sometimes, they have walled compounds with reinforced concrete observation posts. On the 26th of July 1953, the young Cuban revolutionary Fidel Castro, led an attack by 120 men on the Moncada army barracks in Santiago de Cuba (located to the southeast of the island). Just like the first battle of Kabamba, the Cuban revolutionaries had intended to capture a large haul of arms, to use in an armed struggle against the military junta of Fulgencio Batista. In circumstances similar to the first battle of Kabamba, the operation had been compromised by shots that were fired early on in the attack that had the effect of squandering any chance of surprise.

The Moncada attack experienced a lot of 'friction', much of which is not the subject of this analysis; what is important, however, is that in the attack on Moncada, the Cuban insurrectionists suffered numerous casualties and were repulsed. A few days later, Fidel himself was captured and incarcerated. Yet, this was the unlikely beginning of one of the most successful and inspirational revolutions of the 20th Century. The first battle of Kabamba, the clarion call of the Ugandan resistance war, managed to avoid these set-backs. The attackers of Kabamba were able to impose relative superiority on a vastly superior opposing force. They virtually took control of important communications and administrative nodes within the facility for one hour, suffered minimal casualties and withdrew in good order. No small achievement for soldiers who were still novices at this sort of thing.

What could have been done differently? Lieutenant Elly Tumwine's action at the front gate has come under some criticism in subsequent military discussion of this historic attack. In his autobiography *Sowing the Mustard Seed*, Yoweri Museveni commented that, 'Tumwine should have struggled physically with the man instead of firing at him and that would have given us a few minutes to reach and get control of the armory'[25]. There can be little doubt that this observation is accurate; however, it is unclear how prepared Tumwine was for a physical struggle with the sentries at the front gate. A discussion about this contingency had not featured in the battle preparation when the men were back at Makoole, near the burnt out hull of the armored reconnaissance vehicle. The art of silent killing is not something that is easily acquired, it requires the attacker to know where to strike and with what weapon. Lieutenant Elly Tumwine had no experience with this and could have quite possibly ended up the worse for his efforts had he tried to physically fight with the sentries. Additionally, there is no guarantee that in a scuffle between

Tumwine's section and the sentries someone would not have let off a shot, hence alerting the guard at the armory.

The human body has a number of lethal pressure points that when struck with sufficient force can disable or kill a man. There are at least six lethal pressure points on a person's head for example, these are: the eyes; the ears; nose; jaw; chin and skull. A moderate blow to the back of a person's ears or the base of the skull, for example, can cause unconsciousness. Other pressure points are found in the neck, torso and lower body. Martial arts experts know these pressure points and are adept at targeting them.

Had the men discussed the need to quietly dispose the sentries at the gate, then it would have become clear that someone with martial arts skills was required for this task. If no one with these skills was available, the plotters might have considered an earlier attack, which would have allowed a few of them to creep up on the sentries under cover of darkness. Utilizing knives, they would have eliminated the sentries. The rest of the attacking force would have been ushered into the training school by the knife wielding party, a sort of Trojan horse scenario.

Therefore, not enough attention was given to a deliberation on contingencies. As with the incident at 49 Maluku Estate, there was no consideration of paragraph 3 (Execution) of the five paragraph orders template; specifically, the 'actions on' portion of Scheme of Maneuver. This would have facilitated a discussion of how to stealthily gain entrance into the training school. Once the requirement to dispatch the sentries silently had been identified, the men to execute this should have been selected and trained (probably in the weeks leading up to the attack). Individuals with some martial arts skills would have been ideal (Fred Rubereza who had considerable martial arts skill was stuck in Karamoja along with Salim Saleh and both men would not make it to the bush for some months).

Naturally, the men who attacked Kabamba on February 6th 1981 had a lot on their minds in the days preceding the attack. All preparations were carried out in a climate of fear. In the weeks leading up to the start of the war, Museveni on numerous occasions altered his place of abode to confound UPC loyalists in the UNLA. The Oyite Ojok faction within UNLA were in the ascendant and looking for an opportunity to liquidate him. Sometimes, he spent nights in the homes of supporters. Wherever he went he was always surrounded by a bodyguard of fanatically loyal fighters led by the unforgettable Akanga Byaruhanga.

Additionally, FRONASA cadres had been targeted and eliminated in the weeks and months before the attack on Kabamba. Notably, the killing of 2nd Lieutenant Kamanzi (a graduate of Monduli Military Academy) and three other soldiers by elements of Kikosi Maalum at Makindye barracks. This led to a retaliatory night raid by FRONASA fighters under the command of Sam Magara that killed a lot of Kikosi Maalum officers and men. The Old Testament principle of 'an eye for an eye' summed up the relationship between Kikosi Maalum and FRONASA in the turbulent days after Idi Amin's removal from power. Just like the 'Wild West', only the gunfighter who was quickest to the draw would assure his own survival. Museveni always the high-minded disciplinarian forcefully opposed any cowboy tendencies, but there was no way of stopping people defending themselves from unwarranted violence. Therefore, conditions were not ideal to say the least for the planning of the attack on Kabamba, all the more reason to be impressed that it met with any success at all.

Any contemplation on contingencies would have certainly led the plotters to reflect on the possibility of the armory being staunchly defended. This would have shown the necessity for explosives of some sort, since this was a formidable redoubt. The grenade and anti-tank rifle grenade (that were used in the battle) should have been reinforced with RPG-7V launchers with their shells, as well as recoilless guns. The force of impact of any one of these bunker-busting weapons would have eliminated the heroic Tanzanian sentry who single-handedly thwarted the attack. The problem was the attackers did not have these weapons and they could not risk postponing the operation in the desire of first acquiring them. Therefore, any ambition to capture the armory in the first battle of Kabamba was contingent on gaining surprise, it was critical to the entire enterprise. The attackers did not have the firepower to overcome a determined defense of the armory.

Conclusion

The time has come to put the first battle of Kabamba in proper perspective. Notions that it was an outright failure should be thrust aside. Certainly, it did not succeed in the most important aspect of the operation (the seizure of the armory); however, there were a number of important achievements. The reconnoitering of the training school had proceeded without a hitch which had allowed the plotters to be in possession of flawless intelligence. Operational security was maintained, word of the attack did not leak to the authorities. A number of guns were captured in the attack (although not as many as the attackers would have liked) in addition to a large number of vehicles. Parts of the installation fell into the hands of the assailants until the decision to withdraw was taken, and most importantly casualties were kept to a minimum (only one leg injury). Tactically, the first battle of Kabamba was, therefore, a qualified success and certainly not a catastrophe.

Although its tactical successes were limited, the first battle of Kabamba was immensely significant both strategically and symbolically. The revolutionaries led by Museveni had been involved in a merger with Obote and Ojok's Kikosi Maalum up to that point. This merger was called the 'UNLF\UNLA'; the first attack on Kabamba announced that this merger was over. Museveni's FRONASA disenganged from this union by an act of violence, i.e. the first battle of Kabamba. Kabamba, also initiated the process of building an alternative politico-military center in Uganda. Once it had been inaugurated it became imperative to sustain and expand it. This politico-military entity would provide the environment whence the Ugandan revolution would blossom.

Symbolically, in terms of the history of the Great Lakes region and Africa as a whole, the attack had powerful resonance. Present amongst the attackers were no less than two future presidents of the region (of Uganda and Rwanda) as well as important military persons from those two countries. Both Presidents Museveni and Kagame (and their armies) have had an immeasurably positive impact on the Great Lakes region and Africa. Lieutenant Elly Tumwine could not have fathomed the importance of those first shots he (and his section) fired. Those shots literally pronounced the start of the struggle of the oppressed (and forgotten) peoples of East and Central Africa against the despotic order of the rump-colonial state. Seldom has a battle held so much meaning to millions upon millions of people. Just like the storming of the Bastille by the down-trodden of France in 1789 signaled the end of the hated *'ancien-regime'* and the birth of new freedoms, the significance of the first battle of Kabamba will only be enhanced by the passage of time.

Notes

24. Yoweri Kaguta Museveni, *Sowing The Mustard Seed*, (Malaysia, Macmillan Publishers Limited, 2007), 128.

25. Yoweri Kaguta Museveni, *Sowing the Mustard Seed*, (Malaysia, Macmillan Publishers Limited, 2007),129.

5

Bukalabi: Saleh's Baptism in Fire

'I have not yet begun to fight'
Captain John Paul Jones

Yoweri Museveni had co-opted his younger brother, Caleb Akandwanaho, into the Ugandan resistance at the humble age of 16 years. This was in 1976, when Museveni was still attempting to organize a vanguard of committed revolutionaries, for the protracted conflict he envisaged. The age difference between the two brothers was ironically 16 years, so for all intents and purposes Museveni assumed the position of a surrogate father for the young (and willful) teenager. In December of 1976, Caleb Akandwanaho (who assumed the *nom de guerre* of 'Salim Saleh') had gone along with his elder brother and 27 other young men to train in Montepuez. Montepuez is a district located in the province of Cabo Delgado in the north-east of Mozambique.

He spent two years training with his comrades under the auspices of the recently victorious FRELIMO. During this time, he developed a strong bond of friendship with Fred Rwigema. Fred Rwigema was a Rwandese of Tutsi extraction, who had come to Uganda as a toddler with his parents in the late 1950s. His parents were part of the first migration of Tutsis that fled the anti-Tutsi pogroms of Rwanda in the late 1950s. As a young man, Fred Rwigema developed a taste for radical politics and was soon drawn to the cause of the Ugandan resistance and its leader –Yoweri Museveni. Throughout his time as a fighter and later as a leader of the Ugandan resistance war, Rwigema never stopped thinking about the country of his birth. Although he loved his adopted home very much and was always fastidious about being loyal to Yoweri Museveni, his yearning for an eventual return to Rwanda was undiminished. The two men were the youngest of the Ugandan group that underwent training in Montepuez (Rwigema was a couple of years older than Saleh). They were tall, lanky and good looking; but above all, they developed into excellent soldiers.

In the Tanzanian-led anti-Amin war, Saleh had initially been held back in Tanzania as liaison officer between FRONASA and Maj. Butiku (Mwalimu Nyerere's Principal Private Secretary). However, later he participated in the advance up to West Nile. It was at this time that the young Saleh named the FRONASA column he was in command of after 'the Red Army', out of veneration for the exploits of the Soviet Red Army in the Second World War. Of course, the soldier in Saleh was only interested in the military aspects of the Red Army, he had no care in the world for the politics associated with the USSR; if anything, Saleh was by temperament a democrat and libertarian; he couldn't abide the slightest show of authoritarianism or arbitrariness. Indeed, Saleh would probably have found life under communism unbearable, it was antithetical to everything he understood and cherished.

The outbreak of open conflict in 1981 found Saleh in Moroto (Karamoja), where he had been banished by Oyite Ojok and the Kikosi Maalum faction within UNLA. His crime was that he had rescued his brother Museveni (who at the time was the Vice Chairman of the governing Military Commission) from a UNLA roadblock at Kireka -at that time on the outskirts of Kampala. The Ojok faction in the UNLA had intended to murder Museveni, his wife, young son (now the author) and a couple of escorts at this roadblock. At Kireka (an incident the author recalls vividly) an enraged and gun-toting Saleh dismounted from a speeding car in the company of Fred Rwigema, Akanga Byaruhanga and one other soldier. He proceeded to violently slap the commander of the roadblock (sending him crashing to the ground), before telling the cowering man to tell his superiors that it was 'Commander Salim Saleh' that had rescued Museveni. That statement would return to haunt him, for a few days later he was apprehended and incarcerated at Mbuya barracks. Saleh was badly beaten over the course of this incarceration. However, Saleh's 'never say die' attitude made him fight back and he mauled quite a few of his assailants. Remarkably, Saleh was able to escape execution and even earned a measure of respect from his incarcerators. Eventually, Saleh was released after Museveni threatened to personally shoot Oyite Ojok if his younger brother died in jail.

After the Mbuya incarceration, Saleh was arrested for a second time in Moroto. This was after the first attack on Kabamba on the 6th of February 1981. This arrest was largely due to the fact that he was Museveni's brother but also because his close friend Fred Rubereza (who was deployed with him in Moroto) had absconded soon after the news of the attack on Kabamba broke. The deployment of Saleh and Rubereza in the remote north-eastern district of Moroto (remote at the time), was part of Oyite Ojok's carefully designed plan of removing all troublesome FRONASA militants from the center of the country. Ojok surmised that with these individuals out of the way he would be able to tighten his military grip of the capital and the chief towns at the heart of the country. Saleh's incarceration in Moroto endured for some months before he was helped to escape through the efforts of a remarkable woman called Dora Kutesa (later the wife of one of the NRA's stars, Pecos Kutesa) and a young officer called Katumba Wamala (presently a Lieutenat General and the Commander Land Forces of the UPDF). He was ultimately able to join the fighters in the bush around July of 1981.

In 1982, the NRA formed what was designated as the First Mobile Force (more on this in Chapter 6). Fred Rwigema and Salim Saleh were appointed Commander and Deputy Commander of First Mobile Force respectively. First Mobile Force was initially comprised of four companies. These were: A; B; C and D companies. It was these companies that would develop into the battalions of the famous Mobile Brigade. The toughest and most experienced fighters were concentrated in D Coy. D Coy was a 'Special Force' of sorts, comprised of the best fighters within the burgeoning rebel army.

Some rivalry had developed between senior NRA commanders, with many of them keen to lead D Coy. Often the operations of D Coy (which was a component of First Mobile Force) were led by Saleh, because of the confidence in which the Chairman of the High Command (Yoweri Museveni) held him. This caused some disquiet in the senior ranks of the rebel army. In late 1982, D Coy under the command of Saleh successfully attacked Kakiri. This successful attack animated the men of D Coy and they felt they could take on all comers.

On the 21st of February 1983, at Bukalabi, near Semuto, this self-assurance was seriously put to the test. Reconnaissance on the enemy unit at Bukalabi had been carried out by a number of individuals including Joram Mugume and one Sergeant Kasozi (part of the intelligence department). The positions of the enemy detachment (specifically the enemy's trenches) at Bukalabi were identified and reported. D Coy once again under Saleh's command prepared to attack the enemy. Early on the morning of the 21st of February 1983, D Coy approached the target; they entered what had been designated as the Form Up Place (FUP) and began to shake out into their attack formation. Unknown to them, the enemy had shifted camp (probably the night before) and now his trenches were directly adjacent to D Coy's FUP. The force at Bukalabi was not your run of the mill UNLA Central Brigade unit. Central Brigade was the UNLA formation charged with facing down the NRA armed threat in the Luwero Triangle. The soldiers that D Coy was preparing to attack were a disciplined and experienced lot, having seen action in West Nile; in operations against Moses Ali's Uganda National Rescue Front (UNRF). In the words of Major General Pecos Kutesa, 'As soon as they entered the area, they dug good trenches, cleared the killing ground and took up positions. No noise, no smoking, no chasing of chickens, which usually gave away the Central Brigade soldiers'[26].

As the soldiers of D Coy continued to take up positions in preparation for the attack, they couldn't have known that their forward ranks were smack in the middle of the enemy's machine gun sights. The stillness of the dawn was shattered by the sustained fire of machine guns and Kalashnikovs. Almost instantly nine men were cut down by the enemy's withering fire. Saleh who was in the rear raced forward (accompanied by one escort) once he heard the shooting. He wanted to know why there was shooting before he had ordered it. He was puzzled by the sight that confronted him once he got to the front. Oblivious to the murderous fire that was raking the ground around him, Saleh contrived to arouse the men he saw lying on the ground. He thought they were cowering because of the vicious fire being directed at them, it was only then that he discovered to his horror that they were all dead. The situation hadn't completely sunk in when he was hurled to the ground by three shots that shattered both his arms. Two bullets ripped through his right arm and one bullet almost tore off his left forearm. He lay there in a bloody mess, calmly noting that the two bones of his left forearm had been completely severed and it was only the shreds of skin around the bones that kept his forearm from being completely amputated. Large chunks of skin hung loosely from his right forearm as well. The pain must have been excruciating. Saleh noticed that the man who had shot him was dead, killed by his loyal escort. Suddenly, he was yanked sharply by the collar to the rear; he looked up to see it was Rwabwisho (one of the rebel army's most daring soldiers) pulling him out of harm's way.

The terrible attrition that D Coy had suffered up to this point in the battle (with nine dead and several men injured) affected the unit's morale and by the time Rwabwisho managed to drag Saleh out of the enemy's 'beaten zone' or field of fire, D Coy had started withdrawing. In other words, D Coy had 'culminated' (as you would say in proper military speak); meaning, that it had reached a point where it could not continue the offense/attack and had to revert to another form of operation, i.e. withdrawal. Saleh managed to pick himself up although he was bleeding profusely and in agonizing pain. He started running after the rest, they ran through a number of valleys; at one point as he was running his left little finger got caught in some shrubbery. Saleh was unable to remove this finger from the twigs it had gotten entangled in, because the bones in this arm had been completely fractured. He stood there motionless, with his finger in the shrubs as men raced past him wondering what he was up to. Finally, one of the soldiers who was running by called Kasaasira (who was once an escort of Museveni) asked him, 'Afande what on earth are you doing standing there?' Saleh responded, 'but can't you guys see that my finger is caught in this bush?' Kasaasira helped him disentangle his finger and both men then ran to join the rest.

They got to a road and a jeep was brought to help transport the wounded back to the NRA camp. Saleh was carried and placed in the jeep; the jeep drove off in the direction of Semuto town. Once it got there it stopped for awhile and civilians mobbed it all inquiring as to the condition of Saleh, many of them were in tears. They asked Saleh what they could get for him to ease the pain and he asked for a cigarette. 'It was the best cigarette I ever smoked in all my life', he was to recall when the author interviewed him. He took a few long hard drags on that cigarette and then blacked out.

The casualties D Coy had suffered had thrown the rebel army into some pandemonium. It is said that when Fred Rwigema saw his best friend lying unconscious in the camp after the battle he broke down and wept, evidence indeed of the remarkable friendship of these two heroes. Saleh had been wearing a jacket that morning; when it was examined later on it was found to have had over 30 bullet holes in it. It had been a miracle that he had not been killed that day and that he was able to make a quick recovery from the grievous wounds he suffered.

Analysis

Bukalabi was one of the nastiest encounters the rebel army had during the war. In terms of casualties suffered, Mbarara (where 45 men were killed) was the worst for the NRA. This is a remarkable achievement for an insurgent force and only exemplifies the extreme precaution that the NRA took in preparing for every engagement. In comparison, the UPDF in its counter-insurgency battles (from 1986-2005) against a multitude of rebel groups (including the LRA) would many times chalk up victories where the enemy would lose hundreds, even thousands of fighters.

The Bukalabi reversal colored the attitude of some NRA commanders towards the development and utilization of Special Forces. Such talk would elicit a negative reaction from senior commanders who remembered the pain that D Coy endured. This emotion is understandable, but just like the NRA did not cease to fight after Bukalabi, the development of Special Forces within the UPDF must continue, guided always by the experiences of the past. What would have become of the world if the Allies (the US USSR and UK) had capitulated to the Axis after the reversals in France, Malaysia, Singapore, Kiev and Pearl Harbor?

Clausewitz's assertion that defense is the stronger form of warfare (as compared to the offense) was certainly vindicated at Bukalabi. Clausewitz had said, 'So in order to state the relationship precisely, we must say that the defensive form of warfare is intrinsically stronger than the offensive'[27]. Clausewitz qualifies his position by arguing that although defense is the stronger form of warfare, its purpose is negative i.e. the preservation of friendly forces; whereas the purpose of the offense is a positive one, i.e. the conquest of the enemy. He cautioned that defense should only be used as long as ones weak condition persists, thereafter, offensive operations should be resumed. He stated, 'If defense is the stronger form of war, yet has a negative object, it follows that it should be used only so long as weakness compels, and be abandoned as soon as we are strong enough to pursue a positive object. When one has used defensive measures successfully, a more favorable balance of strength is usually created; thus, the natural course in war is to begin defensively and end by attacking. It would therefore contradict the very idea of war to regard defense as its final purpose....'[28]

It is fascinating that the NRA was attacking entrenched enemy positions this early in the war. This says something about the inherently offensive ethos of the rebel army from its earliest days. Strategically, they might have been on the defensive as guerrillas, but tactically they were always taking the fight to the enemy. In this regard, ambushes were the forte of the rebel army. It is even more interesting that senior NRA commanders were in competition to lead these dangerous missions. It seems there was no lack of offensive spirit and aggression amongst many of the rebel commanders.

What could have been done differently? The glaring error of the Bukalabi attack is that no reconnaissance was carried out immediately prior to the attack. Essentially, D Coy's mission was a deliberate attack on the enemy unit at Bukalabi. However, before the attack commenced whilst D Coy approached the target, they were effectively a fighting patrol. D Coy was patrolling up to the point it entered the Form Up Place (FUP) and hence should have executed the normal precautions of a patrol. They should have established rendezvous points (RVs) along the route as they marched. These would have acted as rallying points in the event they were ambushed enroute to the objective. Once they were close to the target (say a few hundred meters), the company should have formed a 360 degree perimeter defense and sent a reconnaissance team forward to observe the target. The commander normally leads this reconnaissance team and hence it is called a 'leader's recce'.

The purpose of the leader's recce is to afford the commander an opportunity to observe the target (having probably not participated in earlier reconnaissance) and refine his plan for attack. However, the leader's recce is especially meant to guarantee against the kind of changes in the enemy's disposition that led to the mauling at Bukalabi. This is a critical point and requires the closest attention. I recall a company exercise we conducted in Nakasongola years ago. The final portion of the exercise involved a deliberate attack on an enemy camp the directing staff (DS) had put together. The attack was supposed to commence at dawn. I was the company commander for that exercise and the night before we managed to recce the target without the knowledge of the DS. The information we gleaned from the reconnaissance helped me refine my plan and the orders that I gave my platoon commanders. As we approached the target in the wee hours of the following day, my mind was focused on making sure the attack went in on time. As we got closer to the objective, one of the DS approached me in the dark and suggested that I send another recce element (it seems they had detected our 'illegal' recce hours before and had made changes) forward to check on the enemy. Looking at my watch and sweating profusely, I agreed. The attack went in on time and was flawless; the company attack exceeded all the expectations of the DS. However, it was only later that I realized the wisdom of that instructor who insisted that I dispatch a recce element forward minutes before we attacked.

Once the commander has satisfied himself of the enemy's situation, he emplaces certain elements of the recce team (principally support weapons) to secure the FUP and returns to collect the rest of the force. If there is a requirement, he alters his orders once he gets back to the main force (still waiting in an all round defensive posture), i.e. he calls a quick orders group (O Group) and disseminates the changes.

D Coy seems to have disregarded these standard practices. They might have been overly confident (especially after the victory at Kakiri) and impatient for an easy victory. This was not to be and D Coy suffered its worst casualties. War really is the realm of [danger, uncertainty and chance] as Clausewitz proclaimed centuries ago. The student of war should never forget it.

Additionally, the use of indirect fire to smother the machine guns might have been effective. Had D Coy utilized mortars to break up the fire that was cutting swathes through the rebel ranks, it might have regained the initiative. The lack of indirect fire was an unfortunate feature of NRA warfare. This was principally due to the fact that the rebel army lacked adequate indirect fire assets and even when they captured a few mortars they lacked experienced crew to employ them. This deficiency in artillery reinforces the notion that the Ugandan resistance war had to cope without the copious amounts of indirect firepower emblematic of campaigns founded on attrition.

Conclusion

Bukalabi represented a setback for the NRA but one they quickly recovered from. Months after the thrashing they got at Bukalabi, First Mobile Force under Fred Rwigema and Salim Saleh were meting out vengeance on the UNLA at Luwero. Saleh who had not yet recovered fully from the wounds he suffered at Bukalabi, participated in the attacks with his arms in bandages. If the UNLA thought Bukalabi had disabled the NRA's foremost field commander, they were woefully wrong. Bukalabi had only earned them the implacable hostility of Salim Saleh, a name they would come to dread. Saleh's war with the UNLA had not yet begun.

Notes

26. Pecos Kutesa, *Uganda's Revolution 1979-1986*, How I Saw It, (Kampala, Fountain Publishers Ltd, 2008), 149
27. Carl Von Clausewitz, *On War*, (New York, Princeton University Press, 1993), 428
28. Carl Von Clausewitz, *On War*, (New York, Princeton University Press, 1993), 428-429

6

Masindi: Mobile Brigade Transforms the War

'Maneuver theory, on the other hand, attempts to defeat the enemy through means other than simple destruction of his mass'
Robert Leonhard

Three and half months after Bukalabi, First Mobile Force under Stanley Muhangi and Levi Karuhanga attacked Kiboga on the Kampala-Hoima road and killed 30 UNLA soldiers. They also captured 49 rifles along with other armaments (including 4 mortars) and 20,000 rounds of ammunition. Then on the 16th of July 1983, First Mobile Force under Fred Rwigema and Salim Saleh attacked Luwero killing a large number of enemy soldiers and capturing 24 rifles.

As was mentioned above, in 1982 Yoweri Museveni, the Chairman of the High Command (CHC) of the National Resistance Army, had formed the First Mobile Force. First Mobile Force was commanded by two celebrated commanders of the resistance war, Fred Rwigema and Salim Saleh. The formation of this unit represented a desire on the part of the CHC to see the war evolve beyond a guerrilla campaign. Classical Maoist people's war strategy envisaged that there were three stages to a revolutionary armed struggle. These were: guerrilla warfare; mobile warfare; and conventional warfare.

In the first phase, the revolutionary force is on the strategic back foot (i.e. on the strategic defensive), parrying the blows of the reactionary regime which is on the offensive. There are two ways the revolutionary force survives this phase; these are by nurturing a close bond with the population and guerrilla warfare. Both measures ensure the revolutionaries survive and carefully husband their forces. In the second phase, a situation of strategic stalemate develops as the enemy becomes increasingly dispersed and immobile (due to the guerrilla campaign) and the revolutionaries expand their control of the countryside. In this phase, the revolutionary force increasingly complements its guerrilla campaign with mobile warfare. Mobile warfare is waged by regular military units (as compared to the guerrilla units) and targets the enemy's vulnerabilities, i.e. his unprotected rear areas, or unprepared garrisons. In the third stage with the enemy increasingly confined to the urban areas, the revolutionary force launches a strategic counteroffensive and terminates the conflict. This phase is characterized by positional/conventional warfare.

In the case of the Ugandan resistance war, there was a stage that preceded the launching of the guerrilla warfare phase; this was characterized by clandestine operations (as with the 49 Maluku incident). Curiously, this phase was the longest of the entire struggle (lasting from 1971-1978). In this phase Ugandan patriots were mainly organizing to establish base areas inside the country from which to launch a guerrilla struggle. Similarly, the Vietminh had to initiate their own national liberation struggle with armed propaganda teams, whose purpose was to mobilize the population (mainly through plays and other performances that echoed the communist party position) in preparation for the armed struggle. Therefore, in our experience there were four phases to the resistance war.

The chart below illustrates the duration (in years) of each of the four phases of people's war in the Ugandan experience.

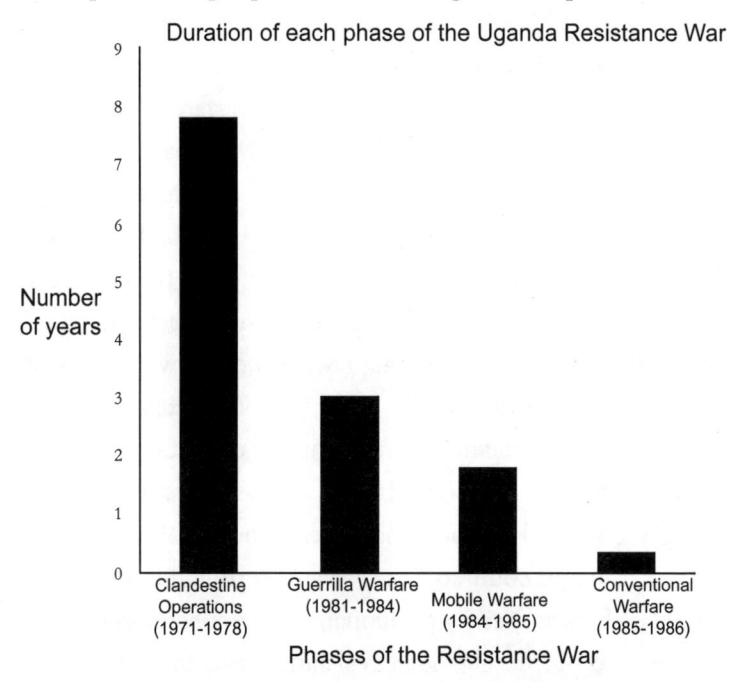

Duration of each phase of the Uganda Resistance War

Phase	Number of years
Clandestine Operations (1971-1978)	8
Guerrilla Warfare (1981-1984)	3
Mobile Warfare (1984-1985)	2
Conventional Warfare (1985-1986)	0.5

Phases of the Resistance War

As the chart clearly demonstrates the clandestine operations phase was the longest by a good deal. It lasted from almost immediately after Idi Amin's coup, until the invasion of the Kagera Salient in October 1978. The shortest phase of the Ugandan Resistance War was the conventional warfare phase. This phase began in August of 1985 and ended with the capture of Kampala in January of 1986. About 5 months in all.

Yoweri Museveni had been reconnoitering Masindi Artillery School since 1982. He utilized a number of individuals on these missions. They included Kaka (an intelligence officer during the resistance war and now retired) and John Mugume (now a Brigadier in the UPDF). Kaka had managed to recruit a gardener in the barracks; this agent was able to describe the routine of the installation during the day. However, the CHC was not satisfied, he needed to know the dispositions of troops within the barracks during the hours of darkness and especially at first light (the hour of attack for the NRA). John Mugume's task was to ascertain this.

John Mugume (or 'Mugume Chagga' as he is popularly known in the army) had joined the NRA in February of 1982; like many others who joined the resistance war in the early 1980s, he had participated in the Tanzanian led anti-Amin war of 1978-79. After the war he was involved in the re-organization that took place in Kabamba and Mubende. He vividly recalls the skirmishes that transpired between Kikosi Maalum based in Mubende and FRONASA based in Kabamba. These clashes were 'serious' in Mugume's words, with members of the two organizations seeking refuge where their force seemed to have a numerical advantage. After this re-organization (which was principally meant to emasculate FRONASA as was noted in Chapter 4), Mugume was sent to attend a junior non-commissioned officer's course in Jinja. He was a contemporary of leading soldiers of the resistance war like Patrick Lumumba and Stanley Muhangi. Both Lumumba and Muhangi left to join the resistance struggle while Mugume was still training. Salim Saleh's officer's course at Jinja preceded Mugume's own course by a few months. Once he was through, he was deployed in the UNLA's 15th Battalion. He was appointed a company sergeant major (CSM).

For John Mugume the reasons that led to the resistance war are patently obvious. 'The UNLA had deep structural problems,' he told the author when he was interviewed. 'These structural problems were caused by a deeply sectarian and primitive ideology'. 'Imagine if you will, a senior NCO calling his company to parade and addressing those members of the company from the southern portion of the country thus '*sikia nyinyi nyote, tutawachinja kutoka Jinja hadi Kisoro. Muta lia kama kondoo* (hear ye all, we shall slaughter you from Jinja to Kisoro. You'll squeal like lambs)'. 'There is no doubt that the UNLA through this primitive ideology recruited for the NRA', Mugume reflected. This sectarian viewpoint was shared by the overwhelming majority within Kikosi Maalum.

For Mugume, this was starkly brought into focus when he won an award in Jinja (at the junior NCO course). The recipients were meant to receive their prizes from the hand of none other than Milton Obote assisted by the Chief of Staff of the army, Oyite Ojok. When Mugume marched forward to receive his award he could not fail to notice the questioning countenances of the two men. 'Even when I marched back to the lines, I noticed them take a few minutes to discuss who I was,' he recalled. When you see your Chief of Staff and soon to be President discussing your ethnicity you know you don't belong, you start thinking of alternatives', Mugume said.

When he finally managed to link up with the NRA in early 1982, he was deployed in First Mobile Force. Fred Rwigema (who was the commander of the force at the time) must have noticed Mugume's leadership skills and soon started deploying him and a few others on what can only be called 'special operations'. They would detach from the main force and penetrate deep behind enemy lines to disrupt enemy activity and movement. 'We used to call them sniping operations', he told the author. 'Our purpose was threefold: first we were to inflict casualties on the enemy; second we were to act as forward outposts of the rebel force (delaying enemy advances into our territory); and third we were to create an effect within the enemy's mind of our ubiquitousness. We wanted him to think we were everywhere and could strike him anywhere. They would think we were more than we actually were.' It was dangerous and painstaking work but Mugume's independent streak, intelligence and capacity to be patient were suited to this line of work.

It was not long before Yoweri Museveni noticed these qualities and started deploying Mugume on reconnaissance missions. By the time the rebel army supremo was thinking of an attack on Masindi, Mugume's reconnaissance skills were considerable. Mugume reconnoitered Masindi barracks two times, once with Kaka and a second time with Peter Kerim, who acted as his radio man. Peter Kerim is now a retired Brigadier of the UPDF. On this second mission, Mugume displaying his characteristic boldness and daring entered the barracks using one of the paths soldiers used to go to drink. It was dark and Mugume did not hesitate to respond to the greetings of the inebriated soldiers he encountered. He was able to map out the internal geography of the barracks, determining that in the hours of darkness the entire facility was completely unguarded. 'I walked through the accomodation of the garrison at Masindi and could hear them snoring, confident in the knowledge that the sentries were alert. However, after 9.30 pm the sentries that guarded the perimeter would abandon their posts and either go to drink or go and sleep. It was a shambles.' Mugume was to return a third and final time to Masindi as guide to the attacking force.

By the latter part of 1983, First Mobile Force had grown into a brigade and was re-designated Mobile Brigade; it was comprised of 1st, 3rd and 5th Battalions. It had also carried out a number of successful attacks like the attack on Luwero town on the 16th of July 1983. At the beginning of 1984, Yoweri Museveni called a meeting of Mobile Brigade's commanders. The command of the brigade had changed slightly since the attack on Luwero. Fred Rwigema had been re-assigned and his deputy Salim Saleh had assumed command. The battalion commanders were: Pecos Kutesa (1st Battalion); Patrick Lumumba (3rd Battalion); and Stephen Kashaka (5th Battalion). At this first planning meeting the CHC only told the men that there was going to be an 'operation'. He wanted to know the combat readiness of the brigade. What was the operational strength of the battalions (i.e. the fighting strength)? What was the status of weapons and ammunition? Once the commanders had answered the CHC's questions they were instructed to prepare the brigade to move. The sick and those with other complications were assigned light duties at the base area.

Mobile Brigade under the command of the towering and handsome Salim Saleh (known to his adoring troops as 'Rufu', which means 'death') then parted with the CHC and moved to a concentration area in Ngoma. There the planning continued and the brigade commander held a number of briefings with his commanders (up to platoon level). John Mugume and Kaka who had both been on reconnaissance missions of the target joined these briefings (so that questions could be asked of them). Stephen Kashaka (who had joined FRONASA at the close of the anti-Amin war, then joined the resistance army in March of 1981) remembers that Saleh conducted these briefings and utilized a sand model of the Masindi Garrison as a visual aid. All these briefings were verbal; no papers were used for fear that they may fall into the hands of the enemy if commanders were captured. A combat leader in the NRA had to have an almost photographic memory because all orders were verbal and there was hardly any use of maps; so if one got separated from their unit, they had to rely on the verbal instructions received during briefings. The price for not listening intently was often very high.

The senior commanders of the Mobile Brigade were not overly concerned with OPSEC (by this point in time) because the bonds of trust between members of the brigade were extremely strong. Everyone was personally committed to the success of the enterprise and everyone knew the price for treachery (*kupinga*) in the NRA was exceedingly high. Spies and traitors (*vipingamizi*) could expect to pay with their lives for compromising the security of the rebel army.

The briefings were conducted over the course of a few days (2 days at most); in addition to these planning meetings the brigade had to prepare the dry rations (comprised of smoked meat) for the expedition. Then the brigade moved out of the Ngoma-Wakyato peninsula (so called because of three rivers that surround this territory, these are: the Mayanja; Lugogo; and Kafu). They moved rapidly avoiding UNLA encampments at Bulyamishenyi and Biduku. They then crossed River Mayanja only 2 kilometers from the UNLA detachment at Buhanku (this took the brigade about 6 hours); then they marched on and crossed River Kafu entering Masindi District. It had dawned by this point and the brigade took a break. The area through which they marched was depopulated and the tall grasses had been burnt (as is the custom in the dry season), what is called '*oruhiira*' in Runyankore. Therefore, movement of troops during the day would not raise suspicions and would be swift. That afternoon they raced towards the target, they got to the populated strip of territory near Masindi town in the night and had taken up attack positions around Masindi Artillery School by around 2.00 am on the night of February 20th 1984.

Kashaka (now a Brigadier in the UPDF) remembers that they moved rapidly and had invested the garrison at Masindi in 48 hours. 'The plan of attack centered on an approach march that did not arouse the suspicions of the enemy; we had to get to our respective lines of departure (LDs) without being detected' recalled Brigadier Kashaka when interviewed by the author. 'We were able to achieve this and it was very gratifying for some of us', the Brigadier reminisced. 'The leadership of the brigade realized that of all the principles of war, the Masindi operation would rely on surprise, speed and security most of all', said Brigadier Kashaka. The Mobile Brigade succeeded in moving undetected by largely conducting night marches; in Milton Obote's Uganda, people did not mill about after dark because of the all pervasive sense of insecurity. 'In fact it was only soldiers that moved around at night, so whoever bumped into us in the dark assumed we were UNLA', continued Kashaka. By 2.00 am on the night of 20th February 1984 the Mobile Brigade had invested Masindi Artillery School and Masindi town. A force under Peter Kerim had been given the task of attacking Masindi town.

In keeping with the plan (and with NRA SOPs) the attack was supposed to commence at first light. Since East Africa bestrides the Equator first and last light don't change. Dawn is always at about 6.30 am and dusk can be counted on to set in at about 7.30 pm. You can set your watch by it (except sometimes in the rainy season when dark storm clouds blot out the sun or hasten the onset of night). The battalions waited in their FUPs just short of their respective LDs; it was dark and the tension was palpable. 1st and 5th Battalions were deployed adjacent to each other. According to MG Pecos Kutesa in his book about the resistance war called *Uganda's Revolution 1979-1986, How I Saw It*, his battalion 'had taken up position along the Masindi-Hoima road, therefore facing the main quarterguard'[29]. The two battalion commanders (Kashaka and Kutesa) had always been close friends and sat together in the dark waiting out the hours before H-hr. At around 5.30 am, a soldier emerged from the barracks (seeking to answer nature's call) and unwittingly walked straight into the rebel lines. He continued to walk unaware that hundreds of armed men were watching his every move.

Eventually, he got to where Kashaka and Kutesa sat; suddenly he made out their frames in the dark and asked in a startled voice *'nyinyi watu gani?'* meaning essentially 'who goes there?' Kashaka and Kutesa tried to allay his fears by telling him all was well and he should come over to where they sat. This only served to heighten his sense of fear and he began to backtrack. Both Kutesa and Kashaka realized that the entire operation hung in the balance, if the man ran he would alert the garrison and the whole enterprise would be torpedoed. Pecos Kutesa, decisive as always shouted *'aya sisi ni wayekera na tume kuja kuwa wuwa!'* meaning 'alright, we are the rebels and we have come to kill you lot!' The terrified soldier turned to flee but was cut down by Kutesa and Kashaka's fire. The attack on Masindi had commenced. Hearing the gunfire around the barracks, Peter Kerim's force opened fire and the attack on the town was launched.

The objectives for 5th Battalion included an armory (Masindi Barracks had about 3 armories), some stores and accommodation. 5th Battalion was also tasked to secure a lofty hill called Kigulya that dominated the entire landscape. Whoever controlled Kigulya hill would have a commanding view of the garrison and the town. As the battalions took up positions around the garrison that night, Kashaka had sent a section to investigate whether Kigulya was guarded. The section climbed to the top and found to their amazement that the hill was completely unprotected. They informed Kashaka and he told them to occupy it. Once the attack commenced, some soldiers attempted to climb the hill (most probably trying to escape) but they were felled by Kashaka's section at the top and by the developing attack of the rest of the brigade, striking from the base of the hill. The attack itself did not take long; after about 30 minutes, the entire installation was in Mobile Brigade's hands. In all, about 40 enemy soldiers had been killed (the rest fled in terror) and Mobile Brigade had achieved a tremendous victory.

The armories yielded a windfall of guns and ammunition. 765 rifles in all and boxes upon boxes of ammunition were seized at Masindi. The guns and ammunition crates lay in a disorganized clutter in all the armories and the men of the brigade did not have time to carefully inspect them before loading them into the 35 brand new Tata lorries they also captured. Only later would they discover that some of the rifles were unserviceable and some of the ammunition they had carried off was meant for pistols and not for Kalashnikovs. Whatever the shortcomings of the operation, there is no doubt that it was a historic and impressive triumph. For the first time the NRA had attacked and captured a huge number of guns from a major UNLA garrison. Additionally, Mobile Brigade had captured the UNLA's entire artillery regiment, as well as a number of Tanzanian instructors stationed at the school. 122 mm Howitzers had been captured then abandoned, because the rebel army had no use for them. The Mobile Brigade had established itself as the iron fist of the rebel army and its 24 year-old commander Salim Saleh Rufu, had earned the position of the rebel army's principal fighting general. The writing was on the wall for the dictatorship and its army.

With their booty loaded on the trucks and with no sign of an enemy counterattack, the Mobile Brigade convoy started for River

Kafu. On their way the, boisterous commanders decided to have a hearty breakfast at Masindi Hotel. They dined and had a few drinks. Stephen Kashaka had his first beer there with his friends. This was the first time in years any of them had been to a hotel. This short break did not last long and soon it was time to return to the unpleasant business of fighting a war.

The convoy revved up again and slowly drove in the direction of River Kafu. At some point they stopped for a break (about 10 km out of Masindi) and a few trucks unwittingly parked under a beehive. The carbon-monoxide fumes from the trucks exhausts agitated the insects and they decided to pour their full fury on the conquering heroes. 'For about 2 hours we were there battling those bees until we were rescued by some of our sharp escorts who burnt the beehive', recalled Brigadier Kashaka. MG Pecos recalled the incident in his book: 'It started with one bee sting, which I brushed away, before the whole swarm attacked. I tried to run to my friends, who advised me not to come near them since they would also be attacked. Everyone started giving me advice on how to get rid of the bees, but the bees were relentless; they stung me everywhere'[30]. The bees proved to be very formidable foes and almost scuttled the victory.

The convoy finally reached River Kafu where they linked up with the CHC who had marched from the Ngoma-Wakyato base area with 700 men to help carry the booty. The trucks were burnt and some of the loot was buried in caches. The buried arms and ammunition were later collected by parties sent up from the base areas.

Analysis

It had been three difficult years since Yoweri Museveni had led the attack on Kabamba Training School that initiated the guerrilla phase of the resistance war; in all that time the NRA had managed to acquire approximately 600 guns. This represented an increase of about 573 rifles from the original 27 rifles that attacked Kabamba. The numbers for the rebel army had grown from 34 to over 4000, but most of these were obviously unarmed. With one attack, the Mobile Brigade had captured more rifles than the entire NRA had acquired over 3 years. The victory at Masindi increased the rebel army's rifles to over 1,300. There is no doubt that with Mobile Brigade's success at Masindi, the resistance war had entered a new phase, the transition from guerrilla warfare to mobile warfare was accomplished on the 20th of February 1984.

In the preparations for Masindi, we discover the seriousness and combat hardiness of the rebel army. The commanders and soldiers of the NRA had been toughened in the crucible of a relentless and merciless guerrilla war. Consequently, they were hard-bitten and more intense than their opposition. Adverse situations are excellent mentors; they compel people to focus on their predicaments and to intently look for solutions. It only took a private meeting with the CHC to indicate to Mobile Brigade's commanders the importance of the operation. Based on that meeting, they initiated preparations, no one (outside Mobile Brigade's small planning group) would have thought to ask what they were preparing for. The principle of 'need to know' was followed religiously by the NRA.

These same hard circumstances had established a level of trust and confidence between the guerrillas so that OPSEC was assured. Everyone knew the dire consequences for loose talk or treachery but things rarely came to that. There was mutual faith between the fighters and absolute loyalty to the cause they were fighting for; after all, once you depend on a comrade to watch your back in a firefight, it goes without saying that you can trust him with secrets. For this reason the brigade commander was able to brief commanders up to platoon level with equanimity.

Salim Saleh must be applauded for utilizing a sand model in his briefings. Today, any military briefing without some sort of audio-visual aid would be ridiculed. The UPDF officer corps trained by domestic and international military academies has come to consider sand models or power-point presentations (also known as slideology) as routine, but not so 25 years ago when we were a guerrilla army in the Luwero Triangle. The importance of audio-visual aids in military orders is evident; many times soldiers are too fatigued by the almost obligatory movements that precede orders that they seldom hear what the commander is telling them. That's why some sort of visual representation of the objective is critical. 'Pictures paint a thousand words' as the saying goes; so once your troopers 'see' that 'this is the main gate, this is the armory, this is the signals room etc' they are more likely to remember their missions.

Once the preparations, preliminary movements and briefings were over, the brigade embarked on its approach march to the target. Mobile Brigade managed to cover approximately 110 kms from the Ngoma-Wakyato area up to Masindi in 48 hours (2 days). This was a remarkable feat by any measure. Usually an infantry formation marching over a 10 hour period (on any march sometime must be set aside for rest) will cover about 30 km, marching at a rate of between 3-4 km per hour. Mobile Brigade conducted its march at night to enhance concealment (except on the last day after crossing River Kafu), meaning, they essentially had one night and a day to cover this distance. At night, marches would commence at last light (approximately 7.30 pm) and end at first light (6.35 am); this means that the brigade would have about 11 hours of darkness.

Once they crossed River Kafu they took a short respite before starting to march again. If we assume they started marching at mid-morning (say 10.00 am) and they got to the populated strip of territory near Masindi about 7.00 pm then it means they marched for about 9 hours on the second day, meaning a total of 20 hours of marching. This means they were traversing about 5.5 km per hour, this figure might even be greater considering the 6 hours they spent crossing River Mayanja on the first night. Thus Major General Pecos's account (written in his book) that they ran most of the way after crossing the Mayanja seems to be accurate.

This feat amply demonstrates the robustness of the rebel army; they were all physically fit (officers and men) and ran mile after mile like the wind. This physical toughness allowed them to realize one of Mao's exhortations of guerrilla formations i.e. 'make a noise in the east but strike in the west; avoid the solid to attack the hollow'[31]. For indeed, Mobile Brigade achieved absolute surprise, while the UNLA was focused on the forces in the Ngoma-Wakyato peninsula (amongst whom was the CHC, who intentionally remained behind to reinforce this deception), they were dealt a grievous blow at Masindi.

The way hostilities were initiated once the garrison was invested exposes the remarkable *espirit de corps* of the brigade. The CHC had instructed Saleh that if he was not able to link up with Kaka (one of the people responsible for reconnoitering Masindi Artillery School) prior to the attack, then he should abort the mission. Kaka for some reason was nowhere to be seen once the brigade got to the environs of Masindi. This would have meant an automatic abandoning of the mission (as per instructions). However, after consultations with the commanders of the brigade, Saleh decided to attack. Saleh still wary of being seen to contravene the CHC's orders told every commander that they would be held personally accountable if the attack was not successful. This display of mutual trust could have only been possible in a formation that had been seasoned by adversity and danger.

Again Saleh displayed that rare quality found in only the choicest military leaders, i.e. of being able to assess a situation for what it is and not for how he would like it to be (a very common failure in many a good commander). He demonstrated that he was a maneuverist commander in the purest sense; his was a 'recon-pull' command style rather than a 'command-push' one. In a command push approach to warfare the commander selects a course of action prior to contact* after assimilating the available intelligence, once this decision is made his subordinates strive to 'impose the commander's plan violently upon the enemy and force the plan's success'[32]. Plans rarely change in a command-push oriented approach to war. In a recon-pull style of command the commander 'refrains from deciding beforehand upon one inflexible plan'[33]. Rather the commander communicates his intent and then leaves it to his subordinates to find opportunities (or gaps) that can be exploited. Once these gaps are located, the entire formation

---

*   'Contact' is a military term that denotes an engagement with the enemy.

rushes to exploit and expand them. Recon-pull command seeks to 'avoid enemy strengths and penetrate his weaknesses'[34].

Recon-pull oriented commanders are cognizant of what Clausewitz called 'friction'. The great Prussian theorist spoke thus: 'Action in war is like movement in a resistant element. Just as the simplest and most natural of movements, walking, cannot easily be performed in water, so in war it is difficult for normal efforts to achieve even moderate results'[35]. 'Friction' is what makes the simplest actions in a peace time exercise very difficult in war. In other words, in war everything that can go wrong probably will go wrong, what the Americans cheekily call 'Murphy's law'.

Having made this evaluation, Saleh devised a custom-made solution for it. Above all, he had the moral courage to allow his commanders to get on with it, knowing full well that if this did not work, he would not be able to avoid the torrent of censure that would certainly follow a debacle.

Ariel Sharon, in his autobiography, *Warrior*, discusses the vital importance of commanders being close to the action in order to capitalize on emerging opportunities. This, of course, is linked to a recon-pull command style. This fact dawned on the young Captain Ariel Sharon in 1950 while on exercise with the army's Central Command. While leading a reconnaissance column for a brigade and with the brigade commander himself nowhere in sight, Sharon learnt the importance of leading from the front. He wrote, 'When this action was over I knew without a doubt that the real commander is the one in front. It's only when you are there yourself, seeing everything with your own eyes, that you can make the necessary decisions, and the more complicated and confused a situation is the truer that is. That lesson stuck in 1967 in the Sinai and in 1973 on the canal. If you are on the spot and personally in control, if you are towing them and pushing them with your own hands, only then can you be sure they will move the way you want them to'[36]. Saleh's command style was unmistakably similar to Sharon's and to other great commanders in military history. However, Saleh, unlike Sharon, seems to have struck upon this realization intuitively and not through an exercise.

Mobile Brigade enjoyed an unusually rare *esprit de corps*. Once they decided on something every part and component of that military machine flung itself into the fray to make things work, there was no holding back, no hesitation, no prevarication. That's why 'the brigade' was such an awesome fighting unit; like the motto of the three musketeers it was 'one for all and all for one!'

The actual fighting seemed to utilize the vital ground of Kigulya hill, which the brigade had dominated prior to H-hour (this was achieved by Kashaka's section). Additionally, by developing their attack from the base of the hill (where the artillery school was located) and driving their quarry uphill, the brigade inflicted the bulk of enemy casualties. Interestingly, this was a favoured tactic of the warriors of Nkore and was used to great effect in the 19th Century.

What could have been done differently? In the circumstances that prevailed (in terms of the life and facilities of the rebel army) at the time of the battle of Masindi, it is difficult to see how things could have been done differently. Indeed, the attack on Masindi is an example of how the intense commitment of an irregular formation can make up for the lack of amenities that a regular army would require before launching an attack, e.g. time to prepare weapons and personnell, time for rehearsals, time to prepare and read formal orders.

Utilizing trucks to transport the men and captured weapons from Masindi to River Kafu ostensibly looks like a bad move. Had the UNLA recovered from the shock of the attack and set an ambush for the victorious rebels on the Masindi-Kafu road, it might have developed into a disaster. The NRA used ambushes to devastating effect throughout the resistance war. However, the reality is that the UNLA was in no mood to put in a serious attack of the victorious rebels. Additionally, the NRA always monitored UNLA radio traffic and would have gotten wind of any attempt at ambushing them. Therefore, Saleh's premonition that the UNLA would not attack their convoy proved to be accurate. The enemy launched a couple of feeble attacks on the rebel army once they had crossed the River Kafu, which were quickly dispersed.

Conclusion

All the ingredients of maneuver are there in the battle of Masindi. It was an attack that sought 'to defeat the enemy through means other than the simple destruction of his mass.' By 'dislocating' the bulk of UNLA forces (the brigade essentially effected a 'positional dislocation' of the UNLA) who remained trying to siege what they perceived as the entire rebel army in the Ngoma-Wakyato peninsula, by striking at a point of weakness for the enemy (Masindi for all intents and purposes was unprepared) and with respect to the rather light casualties that Mobile Brigade and the enemy sustained, the battle of Masindi was definitely an example of maneuver warfare. The victory at Masindi was certainly one a Sun Tzu, or a Mao, or a Rommel would have relished.

Notes

29. Pecos Kutesa, *Uganda's Revolution 1979-1986*, How I Saw It, (Kampala, Fountain Publishers Ltd, 2008), 178
30. Pecos Kutesa, *Uganda's Revolution 1979-1986*, How I Saw It (Fountain Publishers Ltd, Kampala, 2008) 181-182.
31. Hugh Deane, *The Korean War 1945-1953* (Published by China Books, 1999) 115
32. Robert Leonhard, *The Art of Maneuver*, (New York, Ballantine Publishing Group,1991) 185.
33. Robert Leonhard, *The Art of Maneuver*, (New York, Ballantine Publishing Group,1991) 185.
34. Robert Leonhard, *The Art of Maneuver*, (New York, Ballantine Publishing Group,1991) 185
35. Carl Von Clausewitz, *On War*, (New York, Princeton University Press, 1993), 139
36. Ariel Sharon with David Chanoff, *Warrior*, (Touchstone book, New York, 2001), 71

7

The Third Battle of Kabamba: 'The Beginning of the End'

'It was indeed a famous victory.'
Yoweri Museveni

In January of 1983, Milton Obote launched another of his 'encirclement and suppression' campaigns (during the course of the resistance war about 16 such campaigns were unleashed by the UNLA against the NRA). This campaign, which Yoweri Museveni dubbed 'Obote's Grand Offensive' utilized up to 4,000 soldiers and employed large quantities of 122mm howitzers, Katyushas and 130mm guns. In classic NRA fashion, the offensive was countered by an extensive application of ambushes, mine warfare and attacks on enemy lines of communications. The NRA traded space for time and ensured that every advance by the enemy was at a bloody cost. However, this encirlement and suppression campaign seems to have been better organized than those that preceded it. It obliged the NRA to evacuate their traditional base areas in the districts of Luwero and Mpigi and retreat across River Mayanja into Singo.

The evacuation of the Luwero-Mpigi base areas occurred in about March of 1983 and as a consequence of this 1.5 million internally displaced people who were dependant on the NRA for protection (against the brutality of the UNLA) followed the rebel army into Singo. Morale was at an all time low, since the evacuation from the traditional base areas had come on the heels of the disaster at Bukalabi. In a bid to arrest this spirit of despondence amongst the ranks, the CHC organized an expedition to attack the garrison at Kabamba (for the second time, having failed to capture the armory in 1981). 1500 NRA fighters assembled at Nakatete and then set off for what would become known to the rebel army as 'Safari 50'. This huge column marched 320 km to the outskirts of Kabamba; however, the attack never materialized because of discipline problems. Yoweri Museveni writes of the incident thus: 'When we arrived near Kabamba, however, we had problems of food shortages and some of the young soldiers had become rather indisciplined. I was no longer sure that we would not be detected because there had been some delays on the way and some of our boys had run away'[37]. Hence the operation was called off and the rebel column had to walk back the entire distance.

Morale was obviously not enhanced by this episode (thus the name 'Safari 50', indicating it was little more than an arduous trek); however, Yoweri Museveni's willingness to make difficult decisions in the interests of operational success was undeniable. Moral courage (i.e. the courage to make correct decisions, even though they are very unpopular), as they used to teach us at the Royal Military Academy Sandhurst, is always the most difficult sort of courage to possess. 'Safari 50', is one incident among many in the Ugandan resistance war, that demonstrates Yoweri Museveni's moral courage. Of course, morale was soon reinstated by the successful attacks on Kiboga and Luwero in June and July of 1983, as was described in Chapter 6.

Safari 50 represented the NRA's second attempt to overrun the garrison at Kabamba. We now turn our attention to the third succeessful attempt.

Starting in December of 1984, Yoweri Museveni, the Chairman of the High Command of the National Resistance Army, held a series of meetings with the commanders of the Mobile Brigade. These were the same men who had executed the first successful attack by the rebel army on a UNLA garrison (at Masindi) only ten months earlier. The officers and men of the Mobile Brigade represented the finest materiel within the rebel army; they had been forged by years of guerrilla warfare. The brigade was led by Salim Saleh and he was deputized by Joram Mugume. Mobile Brigade's three battalions were still commanded by the competent and audacious soldiers responsible for the victory at Masindi. These were: Pecos Kutesa, Commanding Officer 1st Battalion; Patrick Lumumba, Commanding Officer 3rd Battalion; and Stephen Kashaka, Commanding Officer 5th Battalion.

Museveni related to the commanders that his intent was to attack the large UNLA garrison at Kabamba and capture the weapons in the armory there. As usual, he had initiated reconnaissance on the target prior to this meeting. As with Masindi, John Mugume was at the forefront of these reconnaissance operations. Mugume observed that with Kabamba he had 'perfected' the lessons he learnt at Masindi and considers the work he did there prior to the attack one of his best. The CHC told the assembled commanders that the intelligence gleaned from the reconnaissance missions was reliable. However, he was concerned about the combat readiness of the brigade. This was on account of the increased expenditure in ammunition. In the words of Brigadier Kashaka, 'We spent the better part of an entire night discussing this operation'. Finally, the commanders told a skeptical Museveni that there was no alternative to attacking; the rebel army would require more ammunition for its operations. The operation was sanctioned and the brigade started making preparations.

Just like the Masindi operation these preparations involved ascertaining the operational strength of the Mobile Brigade (i.e. those that could fight). The sick and those who had other issues were removed from the battalions and given light duties in the base area. At this point in time the CHC and the brigade were located in Galamba near Matugga. The CHC had moved the brigade close to Kampala to await the return of a peace envoy, that had gone to the capital to investigate the likelihood of initiating a peace process with the Obote regime. The envoy –Sam Katabarwa- was betrayed, arrested and murdered by the dictatorship. Museveni and the Mobile Brigade spent close to a month waiting for Katabarwa to return, but he never did. The planning and preparations for the attack on Kabamba proceeded.

Once these preparations were over, the brigade (plus additional manpower) moved out from the Galamba base area and took a circuitous route (to confuse friend and foe alike) crossing River Mayanja and getting to Kyamusisi on Christmas Eve 1984. This large force of about 1,400 men included Yoweri Museveni, who was eager to lead the attack on Kabamba personally. By the time they got to Kyamusisi the large rebel force had been detected by the dictatorship's functionaries in that area. Museveni decided to permit the Mobile Brigade to proceed on its own, as he utilized the rest of the force to deceive the enemy as to the rebel army's intentions.

The Mobile Brigade parted with the CHC at Kyamusisi and moved west. They crossed the Kassanda-Myanzi and Mubende-Kampala roads, rested at Lake Wamala and eventually got to Kyahi.

They followed the northern bank of River Katonga, marched through Bubanda and approached Kabamba from the Nkonge direction (using the railway line as a point of reference).

The commanders of the Mobile Brigade cooked up a cover story to disguise their westward movement to Kabamba. They told their men and the friendly civilians they came across that they were heading to Kasese (on Uganda's western border) to collect brand new guns that had just arrived for them courtesy of the government of Zaire (now DRC). This was in case some of them were captured by the enemy and forced to talk. However, some of the perceptive soldiers in the brigade (who knew that area) started doubting the veracity of this story. They started asking their commanders some hard questions. They would say 'Afande, you're saying we are going to Kasese but we continue to march in the Kabamba direction. If we continue with this bearing we are going to run smack into the Kabamba garrisson', recalled Brigadier Kashaka. With a straight face the commanders would calmly tell these men that they were going to bypass Kabamba and proceed on to Kasese.

The final approach to Kabamba took the brigade across River Katonga. They had a *'Muraaro'* (Muhima pastrolist) for a guide. He told them that crossing the river would not be a problem. Saleh had intended to conduct a river crossing in the fading light of the 31st of December 1984, however, based on the guide's advice he decided to conduct the crossing before first light. When they got to the river they found it in full flood, crossing it was a nightmare. Rifles got soaked and some developed stoppages, everyone was frustrated. As dawn approached they were still trying to get the entire brigade across the river. At some point after crossing River Katonga they crossed the Nkonge – Kabamba road. The brigade then advanced on Kabamba on the left side of the road that comes from Nkonge. They approached the target by way of some hills.

Initiating attacks at dawn was pretty much SOP for the NRA, but it was not until about 10.00 am on the 1st of January 1985 that the Mobile Brigade launched the attack. There was a bit of despair and anxiety about attacking in broad daylight, but the unflappable Patrick Lumumba rallied his comrades by telling them there was no going back now, the die was cast, they had to attack! The third battle of Kabamba had begun.

When the Kabamba garrison saw the brigade begin to advance on them they fled in terror. They said, 'The entire rebel army has come to annihilate us!' The rebels walked into an open camp, fighting was minimal. They found the families of soldiers still in their accommodation, wondering what had become of their valiant mensfolk. It was only at the armory where one stout-hearted UNLA soldier tried to repeat the actions of the Tanzanian machine-gunner that had thwarted the first attack on the garrison four years earlier.

The seizure of the armory was one of 5th Battalion's objectives. Its Commanding Officer, Stephen Kashaka, was on hand to ensure that this time nothing stood between the rebel army and the securing of those weapons. At first all seemed calm around the armory; a couple of Kashaka's men advanced to the entrance and did not attract any fire. Kashaka followed to see if the armory had also been abandoned in the panic, but as he walked down to the entrance, the concrete around him started chipping away, as bullets ricocheted off the hard surface. He and the men that were with him doubled back up the walkway. Then it was calm again. He informed Salim Saleh that there were people in the armory. His men surrounded the armory and some began to fire inside. There was a prolonged silence and Kashaka's men began to believe that whoever was inside was probably dead, injured or had bolted.

Two of them, displaying the kind of machismo that was typical of the NRA decided to rush the armory, in order to confirm whether the defenders of the armory were no more. They ran forward, darting hither and thither as they went. The stalwart defender of the armory opened up and shot both of them, injuring them. The men collapsed in a heap at the base of the walkway, they were in severe pain. The lone defender was located at the far end of the armory and could not see them once they fell at the base of the walkway. Kashaka ordered his men to throw the wounded men some ropes and pull them out of harms way. They complied. Once the ropes got to them the wounded men held onto them (each man had his own rope). Then with one mighty heave both ropes were pulled up the walkway, saving the men.

The UNLA soldier seeing the soldiers being pulled out of danger (and having no time to fire) started taunting the NRA soldiers who were outside. He said, *'Eh nime wumiza awo'*, meaning, 'I have wounded those ones'. Saleh who was standing close by started to engage the soldier in a conversation. He told him that if he surrendered the armory to him he would personally commission him into the rebel army and award him the rank of 'Major'. The soldier responded scornfully that he was not interested in joining the rebels. He continued by saying, *'Nyinyi watu muwache kitu yi, yi kitu nia kwetu'* meaning 'you guys should forget about taking these guns, these are ours'. As this dialogue progressed, the men of the NRA's fledgling field engineering unit (led by Kagezi who is now a Major in the UPDF) lowered a bag that contained a landmine inside, at the entrance of the armory. This was the rebel army's insurance policy, in the event that some unfortunate fool tried to repeat the 1981 actions of the Tanzanian soldier.

When the UNLA soldier saw the sack he started to mock the rebels. '*Lakini nyinyi watu muko wa chawe?*' By this he meant 'are you people witchdoctors?' Then he added, '*Muko wajinga kweri, gunia niya nini?*' Meaning 'you are really stupid, what is the sack for?' Saleh, who was beginning to get concerned that reinforcements might be sent from Mubende (a neighbouring garrison) to come to the rescue of Kabamba, told the soldier that time was running out. He had to make a decision. The man's taunts and insults went on unabated.

Kagezi detonated the landmine and there was a deafening explosion. Kashaka remembers that he felt that his ear drums had burst and couldn't hear properly for some time after that. Fortunately (for Mobile Brigade), the explosion did not set off secondary explosions inside the armory. There was silence and after sometime a few of the rebels gathered the courage to descend into the armory and check; once inside the armory they saw that the stubborn defender had been vaporized by the explosion. They were also met by the gratifying sight of a well organized armory. Unlike the Masindi armory, rifles, machineguns and ammunition crates were all neatly stacked in tidy rows. The rifles and machineguns were in immaculate condition.

The Mobile Brigade had captured in all about 650 rifles, some machineguns and lots of ammunition. According to Ondoga ori Amaza the equipment that was captured (in addition to the rifles mentioned) included 'over 90,000 rounds of ammunition, 4 general purpose machine-guns, 1 12.7mm anti-aircraft gun, 1 60mm mortar, 400 hand grenades, 124 RPG shells, 70 2-inch mortar shells and 93 anti-tank grenades'[38]. The soldiers wasted no time in starting to carry off this booty; they also immediately started charging their magazines. Once his battalion was through charging their magazines, Saleh ordered Pecos Kutesa to go and block the advance of reinforcements (from Mubende) who had started moving in the direction of Kabamba. 1st Battalion rushed and occupied defensive trenches that faced the Mubende road and quickly dispersed the reinforcements.

At 3.00 pm on January 1st 1985, Salim Saleh radioed the CHC (Yoweri Museveni) and informed him that they had successfully captured the Kabamba garrison and all its guns, also that they had defeated an attempt by the UNLA to reinforce the Kabamba garrison from Mubende. The two groups agreed to link-up as soon as possible and eventually managed to do just that. After eight days, the two forces linked up at Birembo Primary School, where on the 10th of January 1985 another famous battle was fought with LTC. John Ogole's Special Forces.

Analysis

In the aftermath of the successful battle of Masindi, the NRA had launched a number of operations intended to underscore their continuing lethality as a rebel army. The most prominent of these was the attack on Hoima town on the 2nd of June 1984 by Mobile Brigade under the personal command of Yoweri Museveni.

Other operations included the attacks on Semuto and Kapeeka which were launched by NRA zonal forces* about the same time as the attack on Hoima. In addition, the NRA started reclaiming

---

* Zonal forces were the NRA's regional forces that operated within the rebel army's six war zones. Namely Mondlane, Lutta, Kabalega, Nkurumah, Mwanga, Abdel Nasser (later re-designated Task Force). Their operations were local to those regions as opposed to Mobile Brigade's long-range and strategic operations.

its traditional base areas in the Luwero- Mpigi territories; this led to engagements between the NRA and UNLA. Ondoga ori Amaza records these engagements in some detail in his book *Museveni's Long March*. He writes:

'An ambush at Nsanje on 5 November 1984 in which 5 UNLA soldiers were killed, and another on 9 November in which a vehicle taking wages to a UNLA detachment was destroyed with 20 soldiers killed and 7 rifles along with the pay cheque of 1.7 million shillings being confiscated; an ambush along the Bwami-Kigweri road on 29 November 1984 in which 15 enemy soldiers were killed and 4 guns captured; an engagement at Zirobwe in which 25 soldiers were killed and 8 guns captured; a series of engagements in the Nakaseke-Semuto area on 9 December 1984, during which a total of 68 UNLA soldiers were killed...'[39].

This activity explains why the ammunition stocks had been expended, when the CHC called a meeting to discuss the proposed third attack on Kabamba. The rebel army had been in continuous action since Masindi (really since the war began in 1981) and this meant that ammunition was a precious commodity in the NRA. This also explains why the commanders of Mobile Brigade saw no alternative to an attack, for without guns and ammunition (but especially ammunition) their cause would be in peril. The fact that the CHC revealed his intent to the assembled commanders at the first meeting (unlike the Masindi operation), is an interesting revelation of the level of trust he had developed in them. OPSEC was no longer a cause for concern amongst these hardened men of war.

The CHC's decision to employ one half of the Task Force (that had originally all been meant to attack Kabamba) to dupe the UNLA, was yet another exercise in maneuver warfare. By retaining around 700 men to demonstrate in the areas of Kyamusisi, Bukomero, Kembogo and Kagaali the CHC was essentially 'dislocating' enemy forces by removing them from the point of decision at Kabamba. It was a feint in the classical maneuverist tradition and the enemy fell for it, attacking Museveni's group around the 28th or 29th of December 1984. This feint demonstrates the sort of 'positional dislocation' the NRA used to great effect during the resistance war. We have already observed how positional dislocation was employed in the attack on Masindi (chapter 6), and here we see the CHC utilize it again. 'Dislocation' as we have already seen is an instrument of maneuver that seeks to render the enemy's strength ineffective (chapter 2). 'Positional dislocation' means removing the enemy from the point of decision or removing the point of decision from the enemy. In both the Masindi and Kabamba attacks, the bulk of UNLA forces were physically removed from the battlefield by the rebel army's subterfuge.

By marching at night (another NRA SOP), the Mobile Brigade took 7 days to arrive at the target. Seeing his plan floundering at the final river crossing, Saleh and the commanders of Mobile Brigade did not despair, but chose to attack nevertheless. The Commanding Officer of 3rd Battalion, Patrick Lumumba, is the hero whose propensity to be decisive was by this time becoming legendary. Even while his comrades were pondering the situation, Lumumba would leap into action, telling his brothers-in-arms that when they made up their minds they would find him attacking. French Field Marshall Ferdinard Foch's words during the First World War, where he said, 'My center is giving way, my right is in retreat; situation excellent. I am attacking'[40] are an apt description of Mobile Brigade's fighting ethos.

Junior Officer Class II* Kagezi (the NRA's field engineering maestro) saved the day for the rebel army on the 1st of January 1985. Had it not been for his skills, Mobile Brigade was facing a pretty dire situation at Kabamba. Kagezi and other early engineers in the NRA had received their instruction from Yoweri Museveni, whose training in Mozambique had given him a thorough grounding in mine warfare. Kagezi's demolitions skills ensured that the mission was accomplished.

In effect, Kagezi and his small band of engineers were the 'decisive operation' for the third battle of Kabamba. The decisive operation is defined as 'the operation that directly accomplishes the mission. It determines the outcome of a major operation, battle, or engagement. The decisive operation is the focal point around which commanders design the entire operation'[41].

Since capturing the armory and its contents constituted the entire mission of Mobile Brigade, in achieving this for the brigade, the engineers under Kagezi were the decisive operation. The missions of the other battalions were essentially shaping operations for the decisive operation. Shaping operations are defined as '[operations] at any echelon that create and preserve conditions for the success of the decisive operation'[42].

---

*   The NRA ranks in the resistance war were essentially divided into three categories. Junior Officer ranks, Senior Officer ranks and Members of High Command. Junior Officer Class II (JO II) would be the equivalent of a Lieutenant in a conventional military formation. Junior Officer Class I would be equivalent to a Captain. The senior ranks started at Major up to full Colonel. Members of High Command were equivalent of General officers in the conventional army.

Had 5th Battalion managed to accomplish the mission on its own without the help of the engineers, then they would have constituted the brigade's decisive operation. It's a startling fact, but Kagezi and his engineers were the decisive operation in that famous battle, something that our current generation of UPDF engineers should draw inspiration from.

What could have been done differently? It is difficult to argue with success and since the third battle of Kabamba was a resounding success, there isn't much one can decipher that could have been done any differently. In Brigadier Kashaka's opinion, the reconnaissance for the third battle of Kabamba was deficient in certain respects. It failed to take into account the considerable water obstacle of the Katonga River and underestimated distances. This resulted in the attack being initiated later than had been planned. Had it not been for the decisiveness of Mobile Brigade's commanders the entire operation might have been compromised by these delays. It would have been difficult to try to conceal 700 fighters in the vicinity of Kabamba after the river crossing was accomplished. The Kabamba garrison as well as neighboring garrisons would have all been alerted as to the rebels' presence and purpose. An attack in these circumstances would be costly if not an unwise proposition.

Regardless of the delays, once the brigade attacked they quickly overran the garrison. However, capturing the armory eluded them for 3 to 4 hours. This indicates that the use of engineers was probably not immediately thought of; in fact, all sources agree that a number of other options were tried before JO II Kagezi was finally authorized to emplace the mines. The hesitation to use explosives in the vicinity of an armory (especially an armory whose contents were so precious for the rebel army) is understandable. A willingness to resort to the engineers earlier might have saved on time and consequently facilitated an earlier withdrawal from the objective.

Conclusion

The third battle of Kabamba joins the battle of Masindi as another demonstration of maneuver warfare in the resistance war. Once again utilizing the maneuverist instrument of 'positional dislocation', the NRA was able to isolate the Kabamba garrison and surprise it on the 1st of January 1985. With the loss of the armory at Kabamba, things were increasingly looking dicey for the UNLA. After the 1st of January 1985, the writing was certainly on the wall for the UNLA. The UNLA was facing imminent obliteration and this had been made possible by the NRA's adept application of maneuver warfare.

Notes

37. Yoweri Museveni, *Sowing the Mustard Seed*, (Malaysia, Macmillan Publishers Limited,2007) 156.
38. Ondoga ori Amaza, *Museveni's Long March*, From Guerrilla to Statesman (Fountain Publishers Ltd, Kampala, 1998) 96-97.
39. Ondoga ori Amaza, *Museveni's Long March*, From Guerrilla to Statesman (Fountain Publishers Ltd,Kampala, 1998), 93-94
40. Marsal Ferdinand Foch Quotes, http://thinkexist.com/quotation/the_fundamental_qualities_for_good_execution_of_a/176565.html (accessed May 18, 2009)
41. FM 3-0 Operations, (Washington DC, 2008) 5-11
42. FM 3-0 Operations, (Washington DC, 2008) 5-11

8

Battle of Kembogo: The Enemy's Center of Gravity is Shattered

'Before Alamein we survived; after Alamein we conquered'
Winston Churchill

In late March of 1985, two months after the victory at Kabamba, an NRA column comprised of 11th Battalion, the Headquarters garrison, supportive civilians and the sick, started an arduous trek from the Luwero base areas to Mount Rwenzori in the west of the country. They were led by the dashing Fred Rwigema Gisa (who at the time had been appointed the NRA's Deputy Army Commander). The CHC's intent in sending this column to the west was twofold. First, he wanted to remove the non-effective personnel from the central sector (where he anticipated that the decisive battles of the resistance war would be fought). This removal of civilians and the infirm from the central front, would free the fighting units of Mobile Brigade and allow them to focus on confronting LTC. John Ogole's Special Brigade. This situation was something to be desired, because protective duties (for the large civilian populace in the triangle) were sapping the combat power of Mobile Brigade.

Secondly, the CHC intended to open a second front in the west of Uganda. The much touted 'second front' had been in the offing since 1983 when the NRA retreated into Singo. At that time, Museveni had come under a lot of pressure from other members of the NRA's High Command; they demanded that he open a second front immediately. Museveni argued that it was foolhardy to commit the few arms they then had in opening a second front, when they had not yet fully developed the front they were presently fighting in. In the face of bitter sentiments from some of his colleagues, the CHC was unyielding. This was a hard time for the NRA, the guerrilla army had been forced to evacuate its traditional base areas in the Luwero-Mpigi territories by a ferocious UNLA 'encirclement and suppression' campaign, the battle of Bukalabi had transpired a few months earlier and 'Safari 50' (an action which had been intended to capture arms, in the wake of the retreat from Luwero) had turned out to be a long march with nothing to show for it. Life was hard, food was insufficient and morale was at an all time low. In the face of these difficulties, it is remarkable that Museveni found the moral courage to continue making perceptive albeit unpopular decisions.

They could not have known it at the time, but Museveni's decision to delay the opening of a second front was a precocious and inspired one. Spreading the rebel army thin in its weakened state might have spelt disaster, instead of concentrating to have impact on one front they would have effectively dispersed to become inconsequential everywhere. Museveni, always a cautious and meticulous commander, refused to stake the fate of the rebel army on anything but cold hard scientific analysis. There would be no second front until the enemy in the central front i.e. in the Luwero Triangle had been sufficiently destabilized and the rebel army's strength had been correspondingly enhanced.

After the successful third battle of Kabamba, the CHC felt the time had come to open the second front in the west and assigned Member of High Command (MHC) Fred Rwigema this important task. On March 12th 1985, after briefing Fred, Saleh and Moses Kigongo on their assignments, Yoweri Museveni slipped out of the country. His mission abroad was to try and procure additional arms for the NRA. Additionally, he wanted to mobilize international diplomatic support for the NRA's impending campaign to seize power. Not even the CHC (with his fabled sixth sense or 'fingerspitzengefühl') could have fathomed how quickly this campaign would develop and how rapidly the enemy would collapse.

In leading the NRA's effort to open a second front, Fred was (unwittingly) re-enacting Che Guevara's famous opening of a second front in the Escambray Mountains in late 1958. The Escambray Mountains, which are located in the centre of Cuba, are closer to Havana than the Sierra Maestra where Fidel's guerrillas were firmly entrenched. Just like Che Guevara's offensive in the central province of Las Villas, demonstrated to the dictatorship of Batista the growing power of Castro's 26th of July Movement, the arrival of the NRA in the Ruwenzori Mountains alarmed Milton Obote's regime. Also, Fred's departure (with his column) from the Triangle triggered a series of events that would lead to the most decisive battle of the entire war.

Milton Obote's propagandists were not averse to spreading falsehoods when it served their purposes; they, therefore, seized on Fred's trek westwards. They claimed that the NRA was fleeing to Zaire (now the DRC) after being defeated in the triangle. However, the regime's commanders in Luwero were not fooled by their own propaganda; they knew that their nemesis, Salim Saleh and his much feared Mobile Brigade were still in the triangle. LTC. John Ogole (Obote's principal counter-insurgency commander in the triangle after the death of Major General Oyite Ojok), determined that he would annihilate the Mobile Brigade once and for all.

For this task, Ogole assembled the best commanders (on the UNLA side) that four years of fighting in Luwero had produced. These were: LTC. Kiyengo; LTC. Kirama; LTC. Eric Odwar and LTC. Otim. Ogole organized his Special Brigade into four reinforced battalions under the command of the officers mentioned above. The tasks of these battalions were to track, block, close with and destroy the Mobile Brigade. They were to fix the Mobile Brigade, to make it stand and fight. By this he hoped to annihilate 'the brigade' by the application of superior firepower. It was going to be a clash between the cream of the UNLA and the finest of the NRA.

Ogole's Special Brigade had its headquarters at Katikamu, 2 km from Wobulenzi on the Kampala-Gulu road. The UNLA started advancing on the 18th of June 1985. This movement began in Lwamata on Kiboga road. One of Special Brigade's battalions started tracking Mobile Brigade from this direction. Mobile Brigade comprising 1st, 3rd and 5th Battalions crossed River Mayanja and entered Singo (they had been located in the Ngoma area). Saleh's intent had originally been to employ counter-tracking measures to elude the enemy, but the battalions of Special Brigade were dogged in their pursuit. Once Mobile Brigade entered Singo they were ferociously pursued by a fresh battalion out of Bukomero.

For some reason, Mobile Brigade's counter-tracking measures all failed to deceive the enemy, who tenaciously pursued the main group. Two days were spent in Singo trying to evade the enemy. On the 20th of June 1985, a confident LTC. Ogole dispatched a radio message to his battalions in which he correctly proclaimed that, 'If Salim Saleh's Mobile Brigade is crushed, that will be the end of the war'[43]. The NRA signals corps had developed the ability to eavesdrop to UNLA communications early on in the war; they deciphered this message and took it to Saleh. It seems this served to incense him but he kept a cool disposition. That evening, he ordered his Aide de Camp JO II James Kazini (RIP) to call the three commanders of the battalions. They were Patrick Lumumba, Stephen Kashaka and Fred Mugisha (Pecos Kutesa's deputy). Along with these three commanders other officers of the brigade attended this meeting.

At around 9.00 pm on the night of the 20th of June, Mobile Brigade's commanders had assembled at Salim Saleh's rudimentary lodgings. In the dark of night, a junior officer called Rwabwisho (RIP), the same Rwabwisho who had saved Saleh's life at Bukalabi and was now the rear guard commander for 3rd Battalion, was asked to brief the meeting on the situation. Rwabwisho stood up and brusquely told the gathering, 'You all know the situation' and then sat down. Saleh then speaking tersely told the gathering that they were done with running; if the enemy wanted a fight, then a fight is what he would get.

Saleh ordered that support weapons (machine guns and rocket propelled grenades) be concentrated in a fire base manned by the best men in 3rd Battalion. This fire base (along with the rest of 3rd Battalion) would form the portion of a large L-shaped ambush that would intersect their tracks (i.e. facing the anticipated advance of the enemy the following day). 5th Battalion would establish the other part of the L-shaped ambush and therefore would be at right angles to 3rd Battalion. 1st Battalion would form a circular defensive position about 100 meters behind 3rd Battalion's lines; this is where Saleh and his headquarters would position themselves. Before they dispersed to their stations, Saleh ordered them all to instruct their men to let the enemy advance to 'point blank range' before shooting. 'Let them get to about 10 meters before you fire', he said.

That night, as Mobile Brigade prepared itself for the titanic battle they knew was coming the following day, they could hear the enemy engaged in frenetic activity as well. The importance of the impending battle must have been clear to all the fighters in Mobile Brigade. Before them was a tough and battle hardened enemy; behind them was the River Mayanja and across that river lying in ambush was another of Special Brigade's battalions. The area where Saleh chose to stand and fight is called Kembogo. It is located east of Bukomero and north of Kapeeka. This territory is characterised by long savannah grass interspersed with shrubs. The long elephant grass provides good cover from view, but no cover from fire. On this occasion, 'the brigade' had carried enough ammunition for intense fighting.

The enemy force that had been pursuing them since they entered Singo was led by LTC. Kiyengo and LTC. Eric Odwar. Their purpose was to hurl Mobile Brigade into the waiting ambush of other enemy units that were concealed in front of them. As part of efforts to break contact with this pursuit, Mobile Brigade fought a number of rear guard actions against the enemy on the 19th and 20th of June. JO II Rwabwisho was in command of these rear guard actions.

The enemy started to advance at 10.00 am on the 21st of June 1985, in three columns. The leading enemy component was of about company strength. They were a boisterous and noisy lot. It seems they had been encouraged by the rear guard actions of the previous 2 days, they thought that day would see another NRA retreat. From their headquarters, Kazini remembered that they could clearly hear the soldiers as they advanced. The soldiers of Mobile Brigade maintained battle discipline and let the enemy approach. Then all hell broke loose! Machine gun fire and rocket propelled grenades (RPGs) started to cut down swathes of the advancing enemy infantry. Moments after the firing started, 50 enemy soldiers lay dead. The UNLA's advance came to a bloody halt, they were dazed and bewildered. It took about an hour for the UNLA commanders to get a grip of their forces and to order them to counter-attack what were now clearly visible NRA lines. In the meantime, NRA fighters rushed forward and recovered 44 rifles as well as 5 machine guns (all fully loaded with ammunition).

Special Brigade launched its counter-attack, it advanced on the NRA lines under the cover of heavy and accurate mortar rounds. The UNLA poured copious amounts of machine gun fire in the direction of the NRA. However, this fire was not accurate because Mobile Brigade had carefully concealed its positions in the tall elephant grass. Additionally, Warrant Officer Class II Sekanjako (who was a private in 3rd Battalion's C Coy) recalls that they had prepared shell scrapes in the tall grass and thus had some protection from Special Brigade's fire. This inferno lasted about 2 hours, mortar rounds were landing around Saleh's headquarters. Kazini recalled that Saleh was incensed that his staff had not dug trenches, but in his customary nonchalance he soon lost interest in this line of questioning and continued focusing on the battle. Mobile

Brigade's men remained unfazed by this withering fire, allowing the enemy to advance to point blank range before opening up again with their own devastating fire. This time even more enemy soldiers were cut down.

Elements from 1st Battalion started reinforcing 3rd Battalion's line and together they repulsed the UNLA's counter-attack. Then Saleh's headquarters noticed that an enemy force was surreptitiously advancing on their right flank. They were attempting to outflank the NRA's lines, going around 3rd Battalion (and elements of 1st Battalion) to attack the headquarters. Saleh ordered Kazini to go tell 5th Battalion to deploy urgently to meet the threat. Kazini raced and told one of 5th Battalion's company commanders JO II 'China' Mafundo to deploy to meet this threat. China hurried off with his company of soldiers in tow; Kazini went with them and joined in the fighting. A ferocious battle ensued to the rear of the NRA's lines, a stone's throw away from Saleh's headquarters. The belligerents were only meters from each other, firing at point blank range. Kazini remembered that at this point the UNLA soldiers seemed to be resigned to their fate. 'We were shooting them as if they were bewitched or never knew how to operate their weapons'[44]. One of Mobile Brigade's officers, JO II Kanyeihamba, was killed in this action.

These horrendous losses broke Special Brigade's spirit and by 4.00 pm the enemy's morale was crushed. It was at this point that the valiant Patrick Lumumba started scooting about the lines letting his men know that he intended to charge the enemy. Sam Kavuma (now a Colonel in the UPDF) who was a platoon sergeant in 3rd Battalion at the time, remembers seeing Lumumba zipping about behind their lines, rousing them all for the charge. 'Then at his signal we all got up and rushed them', Kavuma recalled. It developed into a bloody pursuit, 'Our men were all intent on physically laying hands on the enemy' continued Kavuma. Somebody had put out the word that Special Brigade had recently been supplied with new boots; it became the personal mission of every soldier in Mobile Brigade to get a pair. With this sort of aggression, the enemy was pursued as far as Lwamata. Many more enemy soldiers perished.

With the enemy in full retreat, Saleh asked to see Kanyeihamba's body and it was brought to him. Leaning over Kanyeihamba's body, a sorrowful Saleh whispered, *'Kanyeihamba tiwafeera busha'* (meaning 'Kanyeihamba you haven't died in vain'). JO II 'China' had lost a finger in the fighting around the headquarters and Saleh commiserated with him as well.

By the end of that day, the NRA had lost 23 fighters, while the UNLA lost between 200-300 men. It was an awesome victory for the NRA; indeed, it was the definitive battle of the Ugandan resistance war. After Kembogo things were never the same again, for the UNLA it was a 'catastrophe' as Eric Odwar reportedly told an anxious Ogole, in a radio message on the night of 21st of June 1985. Both Odwar and Kiyengo were off air for many hours that night and a worried Ogole began to imagine the worst; finally Odwar sent a terse message to his commander to the effect that [Special Brigade had met with a catastrophe and he would relate the details when they met].

The psychological effects of the defeat at Kembogo for the UNLA were as decisive as the battlefield losses they incurred. Embittered, UNLA soldiers left the battlefield at Kembogo with mutiny on their mind. They were no longer willing to pursue the NRA and the immense losses suffered on the battlefield helped to accentuate the latent ethnic differences between the UNLA's two dominant tribes - the Langi and Acholi. The Acholi were the majority ethnic group in the UNLA, but the choicest positions in the army were reserved for the Langi (Milton Obote's tribesmen). Milton Obote's appointing of Smith Opon Acak (a Langi officer) as Chief of Staff of the UNLA, after the death of MG David Oyite Ojok (who was killed in a helicopter crash, while supervising operations against the NRA in December of 1983) only served to add fuel to the flames of this ethnic rivalry. Smith Opon Acak's appointment came before the UNLA's debacle at Kembogo. This was done against the recommendation of Lt.General Tito Okello (an Acholi officer) who was the Army Commander of the UNLA.

On the 7th of July 1985, these differences led to a shoot-out at Mbuya barracks in Kampala between soldiers of both communities. Twenty days later Milton Obote was toppled from power by Acholi officers and men of the UNLA, led by Lt. General Tito Okello and the commander of the UNLA's 10th Brigade, Brigadier Bazilio Olara Okello. However, the actual campaign to overthrow Milton Obote was orchestrated and commanded by a young (and at the time lean) Lt. Walter Ochora. The ebullient Walter Ochora is presently a retired Colonel of the UPDF and Resident District Commissioner (RDC) for Gulu District.

Analysis

It is curious why the UNLA was willing to take such tremendous risks with a powerful and potent guerrilla movement? Perhaps Ogole and his commanders felt that the NRA would not stand and fight? If this was so, it was a remarkable assumption on the part of Special Brigade's commanders, not only had the NRA inflicted horrendous casualties on the UNLA over the past four years, but starting with 1984, it had proved adept in attacking and overwhelming large garrisons. Yoweri Museveni writing in 1985 described the reversals suffered by the UNLA up to that point in time. He wrote: 'We defeated 16 major offensives of Obote's army, destroyed or disorganized at least 250 [companies] of the same army and destroyed or disorganized 300 vehicles of all types. In terms of deaths we killed more than 4,000 soldiers of Obote's army.'[45] Therefore, it is incredible that Special Brigade could underestimate such a formidable force.

Certainly, Saleh's decision to stand and fight and choice of ground took them completely by surprise. LTC. Kiyengo and LTC. Eric Odwar seem to have anticipated that Mobile Brigade would attempt to cross the Mayanja and return to Ngoma. This seemed like a plausible and probable course of action for Mobile Brigade, in the judgment of the enemy. First of all, by crossing the river and seeking to use this natural obstacle for delaying actions, Mobile Brigade might shake off the enemy's pursuit. Secondly, the terrain in the Kembogo area was too open; it did not offer the traditional protection that the guerrilla army normally exploited. With the exception of the long elephant grass, it was exposed ground, with no forests, no marshes and only mild elevations. In the words of MG Kazini, 'Other senior NRA commanders would have avoided a battle in that terrain; they would have attempted to cross the Mayanja and re-enter Ngoma. It was only Saleh who could have thought of fighting in such a place.' Indeed, it was Saleh's aggressive temperament that galvanized the officers and men of Mobile Brigade and made it such an outstanding military formation. Mobile Brigade had evolved into the sort of military unit that was capable of accomplishing major military upsets. After Kembogo, the brigade indelibly imposed a 'defeat syndrome' on the UNLA.

Although Kembogo is a prima facie example of a decisive battle of annihilation, it is worth noting that it was procured through maneuver. Mobile Brigade essentially lured the enemy into a trap. For three days Special Brigade pursued the NRA, fighting immaterial (but highly exhilarating) battles with JO II Rwabwisho's rear guard. Mobile Brigade's counter-tracking efforts did not pay off and the enemy resolutely pursued the main group (where Saleh was located). In the battle of Kembogo, there were no entrenched lines facing each other prior to the battle; rather, it was a pursuit that fell into an ambush, which developed into a major static battle and finally ended in another pursuit (albeit in the opposite direction).

Saleh's decision to stand and fight was the critical event that ensured that a battle of decision was fought at Kembogo. The Mobile Brigade could have easily continued to shirk contact, concentrated on lethal ambushes (to maul and delay the enemy) and retreated back into Ngoma. The battle fought on the 21st of June 1985 was largely one of annihilation. Starting at about 10.00 am it went on until dusk (the time when Saleh halted the pursuit towards Lwamata). It featured intense firepower (both direct and indirect), was fought at close range with Mobile Brigade being able to hold its position all that day. Special Brigade launched a number of ferocious attacks on the NRA lines that day (after the ambush that initiated the battle), but the lines were sturdy (aided by the shell scrapes that had been dug the night before). Mobile Brigade's pursuit of the enemy from about 4.00 pm till dusk restored maneuver to the battlefield.

MG Kazini's description of the failure of Special Brigade's attempt at outflanking is interesting. Something had happened to the UNLA soldiers by that point in the battle, their morale had been shattered. Their will to continue fighting had been weakened. This has been described as the 'defeat phenomenon' by Robert Leonhard. The 'defeat phenomenon' is essentially a condition that arises once a military force has bungled the intangibles of war. The intangibles of war, or what Clausewitz called 'moral forces', include morale, surprise and fear. The greatest commanders in history have always sought to impose the defeat phenomenon on their adversaries and have achieved this through the realization that armies are little more than a collection of human souls. Indeed, war is a clash of wills between human beings. Men being creatures that can despair and be fearful are naturally unpredictable. Whole armies have broken and bolted in the face of inferior forces because of this phenomenon. Sun Tzu was aware of this frail condition of the human soul and counselled that the morale of an army must be carefully nurtured and preserved. Special Brigade's leadership (and by inference the UNLA leadership) singularly failed in this regard. This failure on the part of the UNLA leadership, led to the 'turkey shoot' that occurred in the vicinity of Saleh's headquarters at the battle of Kembogo.

The pursuit of Special Brigade by Mobile Brigade after the battle is another sign that although Kembogo was definitively an exercise in annihilation, it was also laced with maneuver. According to the late MG Kazini, the enemy soldiers killed in the pursuit were at least comparable to those killed on the battlefield at Kembogo – if not greater. Ardant du Picq, a French military officer in the mid-nineteenth century (in his book *Battle Studies*) asserted that in the decisive battles of antiquity, the greatest slaughter was always in the pursuit. At Cannae, (the Carthaginian general) Hannibal's cavalry employed in the pursuit had wrought great destruction on the Roman legions. In pursuing the enemy at the end of the battle, the commanders of Mobile Brigade demonstrated their grasp of maneuver warfare. Maneuver warfare seeks out the pursuit and exploitation that lies beyond the decisive battle, this is the raison d'être of maneuver in the first place. Leonhard writes: 'The exploitation and pursuit are the only reason maneuver theory agreed to fight the battle...maneuver theory is accelerating toward the fleeing foe'[46].

What could have been done differently? As with the battles of Masindi and Kabamba it is difficult to argue with success. Hence, with the exception of digging good trenches for the brigade commander, it is difficult to see what else could have been done differently.

Conclusion

Without doubt the battle of Kembogo ranks amongst the most decisive in Ugandan history. Just like the famous victory of General Bernard Montgomery's Eighth Army over Field Marshal Erwin Rommel's Afrika Korps at the battle of El Alamein, Kembogo was a turning point in the resistance war. For the NRA, it was the watershed event that marked the transition of the struggle from mobile warfare to conventional warfare. After Kembogo, things were never the same again for both the NRA and the UNLA. In the words of MG Kazini, 'After Kembogo, we stopped being guerrillas, we were free people'. Kembogo had been a battle that pit strength against strength (the UNLA's against the NRA's); in true Clausewitzian fashion, Saleh had [dared all to win all], and as MG Kazini intimated of all the commanders of the NRA, only Saleh was capable of this sort of daring.

Months after Kembogo, the NRA launched a counter-offensive that culminated in the fall of Kampala (the ultimate prize) to the rebel army in January of 1986. By crushing Special Brigade at Kembogo, Mobile Brigade had overwhelmed the enemy's operational center of gravity. This event had immediate repercussions for the government of Milton Obote; in little over a month, that regime was ousted from power by its own army. An army whose strength had been devastated at Kembogo. The UNLA never recovered the initiative and started backpedalling after the 21st of June 1985. In the duel between the UNLA and NRA's elite formations, Mobile Brigade had triumphed.

Notes

43. MG Kazini, The Rush To End The War That Resulted in Negative Consequences at The Battle of Kembogo, (2009) 5.
44. MG Kazini, The Rush To End The War That Resulted in Negative Consequences at The Battle of Kembogo, (2009) 10.
45. Ondoga ori Amaza, *Museveni's Long March*, From Guerrilla to Statesman (Fountain Publishers Ltd, Kampala, 1998) 104.
46. Robert Leonhard, *The Art of Maneuver*, (New York, Ballantine Publishing Group, 1991) 112

9

The Investment of Masaka

> *'I will make them eat the flesh of their sons and the flesh of their daughters, and they will eat one another's flesh in the siege and in the distress with which their enemies and those who seek their life will distress them.'*
>
> Jeremiah 19:9

Events started accelerating after the decisive battle of Kembogo; on the 27th of July 1985 Milton Obote was toppled from power by his own army. The coup makers set up a Military Council (three days after the overthrow of Obote) and this body soon emerged as the supreme organ of the new regime. On the same day, Lt.General Tito Okello Lutwa was sworn in as Head of State. The Military Council started to co-opt different rebel factions that had opposed Obote (although most of them had been defeated by the UNLA by 1985). All these exertions on the part of the Military Council were meant to isolate the NRM/NRA, which the junta perceived as its mortal enemy. They also started to recruit and re-arm in preparation for a resumption of the war. Concurrent with these efforts to entrench the junta, peace talks were initiated with the NRM/NRA. This tentative peace process suffered setbacks from the start because the Military Council was never committed to it. The NRA's response was to re-kindle the war whenever the Military Council showed apathy at the peace negotiations.

In this regard, on the 23rd of August 1985, the NRA went on the offensive attacking and disarming UNLA units in Kiboga, Busunju and Matugga. In western Uganda, the NRA descended from the Ruwenzori Mountains and seized the towns of Fort Portal and Kasese. Then again on the 13th of September, after more procrastination on the part of the Military Council, the NRA resumed its offensive attacking a UNLA position at Kawanda (on the outskirts of Kampala). That same day, Mubende town fell to the Mobile Brigade and 50 POWs were captured. Fred Rwigema's second front in the west of the country attacked and seized Mbarara town (the principal town in the west of the country) but he was forced to lay siege to the garrison there (after a successful counter-attack by the UNLA recaptured the barracks). For two weeks the NRA's offensive thundered on; in the center of the country the Mobile Brigade occupied the towns of Wakiso and Bukasa on the 24th of September. On the 29th of September 1985 the NRA attacked UNLA forces in Mityana, killing 20 and capturing a large amount of arms and ammunition.

As part of this offensive Mobile Brigade set its eyes on Masaka. Masaka town is located about 128 kilometers from Kampala in the south-westerly direction. It is the principal town in the center of the country (with the exception of the capital) and is one of Uganda's larger towns. In 1985, despite the devastating civil war that had been raging for over four years, Masaka was still an important market town for the coffee rich countryside that surrounded it. The town also supported the livestock farming of the cattle keeping communities in Ssembabule, Mpigi and Rakai. Masaka was also (and still is) an important urban center on the vital road network leading to Uganda's western and south-western neighbors. Therefore, the collapse of Masaka and its formidable garrison would open the way to Kampala and to the long awaited victory.

Around the 24th of September 1985, Mobile Brigade began to penetrate the outskirts of Masaka. The brigade advancing from the west (on the Masaka-Mbarara road), with 3rd Battalion in the lead encountered a pick-up truck that belonged to the intelligence officer (I.O.) of the Masaka garrison. The intelligence officer of the Masaka garrison was Lt. James Oketa (now a Major General in the UPDF). It seems Oketa had picked up signs that the rebel army was in close proximity to the town and was carrying out some sort of reconnaissance. This encounter occurred on the Kyabakuza – Masaka stretch (part of the Mbarara-Masaka road) in a valley bounded by a large swamp. Kyabakuza is the last town you encounter before entering Masaka (from the Mbarara direction). Shots were fired at the pick-up, it reversed then turned about and drove off at break neck speed. The soldiers of 3rd Battalion, who were marching in column formation on the periphery of the main road, instinctively went to their knees once they heard the shots.

The brigade commander, Member of High Command (MHC) Salim Saleh, had driven up earlier that day from his tactical headquarters at Rwengwe near Mbirizi; he planned to position himself on a small knoll at Kyabakuza and see how the brigade's advance went. He was concerned that the enemy might use the large swamp that stood between Kyabakuza and Masaka for defensive positions. Once his convoy (composed of three four-wheel drive vehicles) reached Kyabakuza, Saleh briefly assessed the situation before ordering his vehicles to continue driving towards Masaka. The cars drove into the valley and through the lines of 3rd Battalion soldiers kneeling by the side of the road. The sight of their brigade commander's cars driving past them seems to have electrified the men of 3rd Battalion. They all got up and started trotting after Saleh's vehicles. The late MG Kazini (who was driving Saleh's vehicle) remembered seeing the soldiers jogging in two long lines behind their convoy.

The residents of Masaka were initially puzzled by the sight of the guerrilla army entering the town without much of a fight, but soon recovered and started cheering them on. Saleh's vehicles drove in the direction of Masaka Sports Club, which is located in the nicer part of the town (although in 1985 the whole town was a shambles). He set up his headquarters here and started directing the deployments of 3rd Battalion. His main concern was the garrison; he prepared to launch an attack on it. This attack when it came was unsuccessful because the approaches to the garrison had been mined. The barracks also had some heavy artillery and anti-aircraft weaponry. It soon became clear that a frontal attack on the barracks would be reckless and thus just like at Mbarara, a siege of the barracks developed.

MG Kazini remembered that on the first day, there was little activity in the garrison. Saleh and his headquarters staff remained at the Sports Club ensuring that 3rd Battalion entrenched itself opposite the barracks (in the westerly direction, to defend the town from being re-taken by the garrison). The following morning the garrison attempted to advance on the NRA in the town and was repulsed. That day Saleh decided to return to his tactical headquarters at Rwengwe and move it forward to Masaka. As he returned to Masaka in the evening of that day (at about 7.30 pm) his convoy was shot at by anti-aircraft artillery (AAA) located in the garrison. The gunners in the garrison had tracked Saleh's convoy in the dark utilizing the head lights of his vehicles as markers. It is said that Lt. Oketa (the garrison's energetic I.O.) directed the fire of these guns. The fire of the 37mm AAGs and 14.5mm AAGs shook the air around the convoy and rattled everyone. The convoy accelerated to get out of this lethal field of fire. Fortunately, the convoy was untouched and no one was injured. Once they were out of danger, Saleh ordered the cars to stop and standing by his station wagon he lit a cigarette (in his trademark style) to calm his nerves.

As it became apparent to the garrison that a siege was in the offing, they re-invigorated their attacks on 3rd Battalion in the town. 1st Battalion and 5th Battalion had been ordered forward to the bridge at Katonga, in order to block UNLA reinforcements and supplies from reaching the besieged garrison in Masaka. Around the fifth day of the siege, the anti-aircraft and 120mm mortar fire, that was being directed at NRA positions, intensified. Saleh had shifted his headquarters to a house close to the Sports Club in Masaka (which is positioned a few hundred feet from the present day state lodge). Three days later the garrison renewed its attacks on 3rd Battalion's positions. That night the shelling was intense and the UNLA gunners massed this firepower on Saleh's house. Under the cover of this torrent of firepower, the UNLA began to advance in the dark.

At around 3.00am in the wee hours of the ninth day of the siege, the fire (both direct and indirect) that was being hurled at Saleh's house surged. The house was literally shaking from the explosions of 120mm mortar rounds and anti-aircraft fire. The fire from 37mm AAA almost tore off the roof of the house. Later, it became evident that the UNLA had infiltrated a forward observation officer (FOO) in the vicinity of the house, who was responsible for directing this inferno of shells. Saleh was in his room and refused to come out to see what the fuss was about. JO II James Kazini started getting concerned at Saleh's unresponsiveness and decided to go and try to rouse his boss. He found the door locked and knock as he might he couldn't get Saleh to open. Finally, Kazini decided to go outside and see if he could use the windows to see what was going on inside the room. Peering through one window he saw Saleh fully clad lying on the bed, wide awake, with a pistol in his hand.

Flares were going off in the night sky, illuminating 3rd Battalion's positions for the attacking enemy. SO Patrick Lumumba, was forced to adjust his lines in the dark, withdrawing from some forward positions. At about 5.00 am Lumumba dropped in at Saleh's headquarters and was shocked to find Saleh's entourage still at the house. He asked Kazini what they were still doing there? Kazini answered that they could not re-locate because Saleh had refused to abandon the place. Lumumba asked where the boss was and Kazini told him he had locked himself in his room. Lumumba went straight to the room and knocked at the door. He identified himself and after sometime Saleh opened the door. Lumumba, Kazini and others urged Saleh to move to a safer location but he refused. He told them there would be no retreat; he was not going to abandon his headquarters. He also told them they had to repel the enemy's attack.

The firestorm of mortar shells and anti-aircraft rounds continued all night. At around 6.30 am this fire abated slightly, by that time the enemy had advanced to within meters of the house. Saleh was sitting in the lounge drinking tea with Kazini. They could hear the voices of enemy soldiers only meters from them. Saleh kept drinking his tea oblivious of the enemy that he knew was close at hand. Suddenly, a fire fight broke out in the vicinity of the house. There was the sustained fire of machineguns, the staccato of Kalashnikovs firing, the explosions of RPGs and the screams of men being killed or maimed. Lumumba had deployed in the vicinity of Saleh's compound and his men sprung into action once the enemy was at point blank range.

3rd Battalion repulsed the enemy's advance and chased them all the way to the barracks. Having been roundly thrashed, the UNLA did not attempt another attack on NRA positions in the town. They confined themselves to artillery and anti-aircraft duels with the NRA. The investment (or siege) of the garrison at Masaka, well and truly kicked in at this point.

The siege endured for two and half months and pressed the garrison to the limits of endurance. The NRA moved to tighten the noose around the garrison; it dominated all the high ground that lay around the barracks. 3rd Battalion had positions at Masaka Technical School, Bwala, Kako, Kitovu and Kyabakuza. Furthermore, as was mentioned above, 1st and 5th Battalions held blocking positions at the bridge over the River Katonga. Supplies started dwindling in the garrison and no new supplies were getting through the NRA's blockade. The UNLA attempted to re-supply their besieged troops by air but these efforts were unsuccessful. NRA air defense units stationed at the River Katonga and on high ground around the Masaka garrison, would force these helicopters to jettison their cargo long before they got to their objective. Just like the Luftwaffe's futile efforts to re-supply the encircled 6th

Army at Stalingrad, these UNLA supplies started landing in NRA controlled territory.

Inside the garrison itself the situation deteriorated every day. Ethnic differences started to surface and soon became all-pervasive. It got to a point where soldiers were being deployed for guard duty on the perimeter, after due consideration to their ethnicity. Acholi soldiers could only work with fellow tribesmen, the same held true for soldiers from the West Nile region. Those unfortunate to come from the southern tribes were suspected of being NRA collaborators and were simply incarcerated. Soldiers began to respond to and respect orders that were given by superiors of the same ethnic group. The circumstances were not good at all. Men were suspicious, seething with hatred for their comrades, callous and petrified.

The privations of the garrison increased, food began to run low and then vanished. Men were driven insane with hunger, but even more from seeing their families starving. They began to eat vermin (rats to be specific). Rats became an endangered species in the environs of the garrison. People started to succumb to hunger and the dead piled up. MG Pecos Kutesa tells of an incident in his book *Uganda's Revolution 1979-1986*, of a soldier who attempted to forage for food in the vicinity of the barracks and 'managed to break a young bunch of bananas and while trying to get back, was hit in the leg by a mine. His cries for help attracted his friend, who tried to carry him away, only for the friend also to step on a mine which blew off his leg. Neither our people nor the enemy could venture to assist them, not even to perform the merciful *coup de grâce*. The cries of those two mortally wounded soldiers went on for three days before they became silent'[47].

On the 2nd of December 1985, the garrison's will to resist began to crack. On that day, groups of soldiers started to surrender of their own accord. Eight days later, on the 10th of December, the entire garrison capitulated. The NRA took possession of between 2,000 - 3,000 POWs and the armory at Masaka. The NRA leadership decided to hold the POWs at Masaka Senior Secondary School for their own security. The civilian population of Masaka would have been only too glad to lynch every one of them. Eventually, many soldiers of the garrison joined the NRA and many would participate in the final and climactic battle of the resistance war – the battle of Kampala. It had taken two and a half months for the NRA to secure Masaka.

Analysis

The stand-off that developed at Masaka (and Mbarara) between the NRA and UNLA was an indicator of the relative parity in strength between the two armies. Once the UNLA retreated behind well-constructed defenses and employed its big guns it was suicidal for the NRA to attempt a frontal attack. Saleh's decision to lay siege at Masaka after the failure of the first attack was prudent. He was obviously cognizant of the bloody nose Fred Rwigema's second front had suffered at Mbarara (where 45 men were lost) and sought to avoid another incident that would sap morale. Mbarara had been the largest loss for the NRA since the start of the resistance war and, therefore, had become infamous amongst the rank and file.

Yoweri Museveni had left the war zone in March of 1985, before the decisive battle of Kembogo that transformed the war from one characterized by mobile warfare to one typified by conventional clashes. When he returned on the 15th of September 1985, he was concerned that Rwigema and Saleh had overextended themselves. He was convinced by Saleh that they could hold on to the ground they had gained. The CHC's apprehension was vindicated by the fact that the NRA was unable to achieve quick victories both at Masaka and Mbarara.

So both at Mbarara and Masaka, the war developed into a test of wills; they say necessity is the mother of invention, in both battles the NRA clearly 'needed' victories more than the UNLA. The NRA was hungry for success, they had no alternatives to winning; it was either victory or death! This explains the seemingly limitless ingenuity of the NRA's commanders, when quick victories eluded them they quickly sieged the enemy garrisons. The UNLA on the other hand was lethargic and lacking in imagination. Nothing typifies this better than the obtuse battles the UNLA fought at Katonga. At the battles of Katonga, the UNLA did not contemplate amphibious operations utilizing Lake Victoria, which could have out-flanked the NRA position at River Katonga. The UNLA could have attempted an 'Inchon' type 'turning movement' of the NRA's southern flank, by means of an amphibious landing in the Masaka area. Yoweri Museveni was concerned about this possibility and planned to deal with it if it materialized.

Although the individual UNLA soldier was not lacking in courage, he was led by lackluster officers. After the battle of Kembogo, it became apparent that the defeat of the UNLA was a matter of time. The NRA leadership realized this and pursued a policy that exploited this factor.

The employment of sieges also highlights the essentially maneuverist nature of the resistance war. Always cognizant that the preservation of their strength was a central canon of guerrilla warfare, the NRA commanders were not willing to fritter away their units on futile and costly frontal attacks. The fact that the UNLA was still a potent military force was underscored by the reality that the Mbarara and Masaka garrisons were impervious to direct attacks. It was only through an indirect attack (by hunger and starvation) that they were conquered.

The sieges indicated that a stalemate between the belligerents had been attained. The fact that the NRA was able to achieve this vis a vis the UNLA (despite the huge disparity in actual strength) is testament to the aggressiveness in battle of that organization. It is apparent that what the NRA lacked in terms of hardware, it more than compensated for in aggression, tenacity and energy. The fighting around Saleh's compound near the Sports Club demonstrates this tenacity. It seems in a situation where military forces are in stalemate, a commander's will to win becomes critical. Saleh, whose command style and commitment to success bordered on the suicidal, certainly had tonnes of will power. When the garrison at Masaka capitulated, Kazini asked Saleh what he had intended to do with the pistol the night the UNLA's attack came close to dislodging them from the house. Saleh responded, 'If you guys had retreated and left me there in the house, I was going to shoot myself rather than be captured'.

The sieges allowed the NRA to build its strength through recruitment (9,000 recruits were trained and commissioned while the sieges endured) and the procuring of arms. The CHC, realizing that a potential impasse would result if measures were not taken to rapidly increase strength, managed to convince President Nyerere of Tanzania to provide 5,000 rifles and 1,000,000 million rounds of ammunition for the NRA. An impasse would have potentially prolonged the war and created a situation where there was no outright winner of the civil war. This is a situation Nyerere wanted to avoid, i.e. a failed state for a neighbor. Additionally, he was concerned by some of the actions of the Military Council, especially the co-option of ex- Amin soldiers and commanders into the UNLA. Nyerere's rifles were the biggest contribution to the Ugandan peoples' cause by an external entity and for this the late Mwalimu Julius Nyerere is fondly remembered by Ugandan patriots.

The new rifles and manpower made it possible for the NRA to form new battalions. These were: 13th Battalion under Ivan Koreta (presently deputy CDF for the UPDF); 15th Battalion under Samson Mande; 19th Battalion under Peter Kerim (presently a retired Brigadier of the UPDF); and 21st Battalion under Benon Tumukunde (RIP). This enhancement in its strength ensured that the battle for Kampala would be one where superior force would be brought to bear on the enemy.

What could have been done differently? Mobile Brigade's inability to mount an effective attack on the Masaka garrison reveals the still undeveloped condition of the rebel army's engineering department. Although JO II Kagezi had shown tremendous ingenuity at Kabamba (in rigging and detonating a mine at the armory), the mines that surrounded the garrison at Masaka proved to be too much of a challenge. The NRA did not have the required sappers and equipment to breach the minefield that protected the garrison. Additionally, the fire from a number of 37mm anti-aircraft guns was a lethal obstacle to any direct assault of the garrison. What would have been required to neutralize this threat was counter-battery fire from heavy artillery, which the NRA did not have.

Yoweri Museveni chafed at this situation and tried to devise ways to breach the minefield and attack the garrison. At one meeting between the CHC and commanders of Mobile Brigade during the siege of Masaka, Museveni suggested a novel method of breaching the minefield. It required men to drive large logs before them (much in the fashion of a lawn mower), the logs would detonate the mines and men could approach the garrison through these cleared lanes. The CHC told his commanders that the technique had been used by the Vietnamese in their own struggle. The assembled commanders led by Saleh (thinking about the casualties that this measure might cause) dissuaded the CHC from this course of action and to their collective relief he relented.

The lack of engineering capabilities highlights the fact that the NRA at this point was still very much a guerrilla (or irregular) entity. It had very little in the way of the paraphernalia of a regular military force. No large artillery pieces, no mechanized infantry, no armored units, no aviation and certainly no Bangalore torpedoes for breaching minefields. The NRA for the duration of the war was pre-dominantly a light infantry force with some anti-armor and anti-air capability. The fact that they won the war in this condition and against a much better equipped (although poorly led) foe only enhances the heroic nature of the NRA.

If Mobile Brigade had possessed the engineering capability to breach the minefield, there probably would have been no requirement for the siege. An attack might have been launched with realistic chances for success. The fact that this was not possible only reinforces the argument that the NRA at Masaka and Mbarara had not built up the military muscle required to engage in a full on conventional fight. Nevertheless, the maneuverist and restless intellect of the NRA's commanders struck upon siege warfare. Siege warfare was especially suited to the Masaka area because of the advantageous terrain, with the town nestled between hills. He who commanded the heights around Masaka commanded the town. It took time but achieved its purpose, the defeat of the enemy.

Conclusion

The sieges of Masaka and Mbarara were another exercise in maneuver warfare, i.e. by 'defeating the enemy through means other than the destruction of his mass'. At Masaka and Mbarara the NRA utilized the gnawing and excruciating effects of hunger to defeat the enemy. A tribute to the brilliance of the NRA leaders who were able to conjure up victories in the face of veritable difficulties.

Notes

47. Pecos Kutesa, *Uganda's Revolution 1979-1986*, How I Saw It (Fountain Publishers Ltd, Kampala, 2008) 224

10

Kampala

> *'I never rebel so much against France as not to regard Paris with a friendly eye; she has had my heart since my childhood.... I love her tenderly, even to her warts and her spots.'*
>
> Michel de Montaigne

Masaka's capitulation set the stage for the surrender of Mbarara's garrison approximately three weeks later. Reinforcements were transported from Masaka to Mbarara, to tighten the noose around that garrison. With the submission of Mbarara, the way seemed to be clear to the capital. Operationally, the NRA had cleared the entire center and south-western sections of the country of enemy units, essentially, laying claim to two thirds of the country. This territory was the most populous and productive portion of the nation. In the process, the rebel army had seized two of Uganda's most important urban centers along with their garrisons. It was an astounding coup considering that six months prior to the victory at Mbarara, the rebel army was still a guerrilla outfit being hounded by Special Brigade in the Singo-Ngoma area. The key event had been the decisive battle of Kembogo where the UNLA's operational center of gravity had been obliterated.

The lightning campaign that followed the battle of Kembogo demonstrated how the initiative had passed decisively to the NRA. However, as both Masaka and Mbarara proved, the NRA had not built sufficient bulk to engage in conventional battles. It was still a light infantry force and once it encountered the heavy weaponry of the garrisons in Masaka and Mbarara it ran up against a brick wall. The restless maneuverist intellect of the NRA's commanders, conjured up siege warfare and prevailed over the garrisons. Led by the audacity of Salim Saleh, the NRA in true maneuverist fashion considered it more desirable to maintain the momentum against a stunned and smarting enemy, rather than pause to build up conventional power before carrying on with the fight. In maneuver warfare, it is an unpardonable sin to halt operations once the enemy's will has started to rupture. This canon holds true whether the reasons (for taking a pause) are in order to re-supply, re-fit or re-man. Once the enemy's cohesion is broken, maintaining the momentum takes precedence over any operational pause for any of the reasons mentioned above. Just like Erwin Rommel at the head of the 7th Panzer Division in France (in 1940), pushing ever further into enemy territory, ignoring threats to his flanks and rear, relying solely on the shock effect of his armored thrust, the NRA trusted in speed and aggressiveness, to crush the enemy before he shrugged off the corrosive psychological effects of the 'defeat phenomenon'.

By December 1985, the re-organization that had been taking place in the NRA as the sieges progressed was over. The new manpower (the 9000 recruits) had graduated from the rebel army's training camps (in places like Buhweju) and had been integrated into the fighting battalions. Sometime before the end of September 1985, the CHC travelled in a long convoy of vehicles (including trucks) from Rwengwe sub-county headquarters (formerly Saleh's tactical headquarters and now the CHC's). The convoy picked its way through Rakai and Rugaaga in Bukanga district. Accompanying Yoweri Museveni was Fred Rwigema; the convoy spent the night at Rugaaga sub-county headquarters. The following day they continued to Nyamarungi where they waited for the Tanzanian consignment of arms and ammunition (promised by Mwalimu Nyerere). The Tanzanians arrived at the appointed time with 14 fully loaded trucks. The delivery was transferred to the NRA trucks and then the CHC, Rwigema and their large entourage returned to Rwengwe. The arms were distributed from Rwengwe; they were used to arm the recruits.

At around this time, it was decided to expand the permitted strength of the battalions. After the third battle of Kabamba the CHC along with senior commanders of the NRA had created battalions with an establishment of 300 rifles. These were the old battalions of Mobile Brigade i.e. 1st, 3rd and 5th, as well as other newly created battalions like 7th, 9th and 11th Battalions. 9th Battalion was commanded by Julius Chihandae (now a retired Colonel serving as a military attaché abroad) and 11th Battalion was commanded by the one-eyed Chefe Ali (RIP), who as will be remembered (from Chapter 3) was another of the Montepuez cadre of commanders. Each battalion had four companies of 75 rifles (i.e. half of its men were armed) each. So by early 1985 the NRA had six battalions with approximately 300 guns each, making for a total of 1,800 rifles. Mobile Brigade's victories at Masindi and Kabamba had made this augmentation possible by early 1985. It was a massive transformation in the fortunes of the rebel army bearing in mind that at Masindi a year before, each of Mobile Brigade's battalions had only 75 rifles.

The CHC's efforts to procure arms abroad between March and September 1985 resulted in the dropping of 800 rifles and 800,000 rounds of ammunition by the Libyans while Museveni was abroad. This was the extent of Libyan support for the Ugandan resistance war (except for 92 rifles and 100 land mines in the early years of the war). The location of this drop was in the traditional base areas of the NRA in Ngoma, at Ruharo's farm. The Libyans used an Illyushin 76 aircraft for this purpose. MG Pecos Kutesa, in his book recalls '[spending] an exhausting day chasing the white parachutes and retrieving the precious cargo'[48]. Some of these parachutes dropped in the vicinity of Wazza hill in the present day Kaweweta military cantonment. An area the author is quite familiar with. The Libyan rifles plus the guns that Mobile Brigade captured in Mubende helped form the rebel army's 13th Battalion under Ivan Koreta and 15th Battalion under Samson Mande.

Now with the substantial Tanzanian consignment, the CHC formed 19th Battalion under Peter Kerim and 21st Battalion under Benon Tumukunde (RIP). As was mentioned above, with the augmentation in arms, ammunition and manpower, a decision was taken to increase the size of all ten of the rebel army's battalions. Normally an infantry battalion's manpower stands at between 500-700 men, depending on the table of organization and equipment(TOE) of that particular army. The NRA expanded its battalions to almost brigade sized formations, with each having approximately 1,500 men under arms. 19th and 21st Battalions had about 1,900 men under arms each. The reason for this was that the leadership of the NRA wanted to maximize the output of the few 'field grade' (or battalion level) officers that five years of fighting in the Luwero Triangle had produced. It was therefore felt that it was wiser to marshal as much combat power under these limited but tried and tested veterans, than to disperse it amongst commanders who were uninitiated.

With the capitulation of Mbarara in early January 1986, events started snowballing. Political pressure was mounting for the NRA to implement the Nairobi Peace Accord. The 'Nairobi Peace Accord' was the result of the duplicitous negotiations between the junta and the NRA. This agreement was supposed to facilitate the formation of a coalition government and a new national army (with equal representation from the UNLA and NRA). However, no one in the NRA was fooled by these niceties; no one believed for a moment that the UNLA had suddenly changed its cruel streak. However, pressure mounted on Yoweri Museveni to honor the accords.

In this regard, President Moi of Kenya invited Yoweri Museveni to his farm in Nakuru on Christmas day of 1985; his aim was to belabor the point about entering a coalition government with the Okello-Bazilio junta. Museveni spent the whole day there talking to Moi but left unconvinced (as indeed was the entire rebel army) that the Military Council could be a serious partner in Uganda's rebirth. For even as the parties talked in Nairobi, the killing, raping and plundering of innocent Ugandans by Bazilio's thugs went on unabated. No one was brought to book for these crimes. So for the revolutionary power that now stood at the gates of Kampala, there was only one way that real change was going to come for the blood-stained Ugandan nation and that was through the barrels of thousands of rebel Kalashnikovs.

Soon after Mbarara fell, the CHC called a meeting of senior NRA commanders at Masaka Sports Club. In this meeting, he communicated his decision to attack Kampala and appointed Salim Saleh the 'overall' commander for the operation. Those in attendance (of this and the subsequent meeting) included

Fred Rwigema, Patrick Lumumba, Pecos Kutesa, Fred Mugisha, Ahmed Kashillingi, Akanga Byaruhanga and Jet Mwebaze. Museveni authorized Saleh to start planning for the attack and to present his plan to the meeting in a few days. Saleh huddled with a few trusted lieutenants and produced a plan. The plan that was presented to the CHC and other senior commanders a few days later called for the investment (encirclement) of the capital by six of the rebel army's expanded battalions. Additionally, there was one task force (comprised of about 500 men) that was referred to as a 'Special Force'; it was commanded by Jet Mwebaze (RIP). In all, about 9,600 NRA troops would be involved in the attack on Kampala. In essence, it was going to be the rebel army's first (and only) division attack and Salim Saleh could add the feat of being the NRA's first division commander to his already astonishing list of achievements. The 17th of January 1986 was designated as D-day, three days before that Saleh had turned 26 years old.

In addition to the role they played in encircling the capital (from the west) four battalions (1st, 3rd, 7th and 11th Battalions) were directed to act as the 'break-in' force. Their role was to first gain a firm foothold in the suburbs of the city, with this traction the NRA would launch operations to secure the main objectives in the capital. 13th Battalion, 5th Battalion and Jet's Special Force were to isolate the city in the northern, southern and eastern directions. The attacks by the break-in battalions would be delivered along an axis that ran from west to east. Attacks would also be developed from the north-west of the city (i.e. Kampala-Hoima road) and would push generally eastwards. Like a piston compressing air against the hard interior of a cylinder, the break-in battalions would drive the enemy eastwards where they would run up against the hard punch of the Special Force (which was supposed to set an ambush along Jinja road).

Once the main objectives were secured (these were identified as the three military garrisons in the city, namely; Lubiri, Makindye and Kololo Summit View, plus the 'information operations' hub of the junta located at Radio Uganda), then the city would be cleared of any remaining pockets of resistance, before all attacking forces would re-organize and re-set themselves for future offensive operations. It was almost the textbook solution to the problem of offensive operations in urban terrain (except for the fact that the investment of the capital in the north-west, i.e. Hoima road, would be achieved as the attack progressed and not before). This is remarkable given the fact that Saleh and his companions probably received little instruction and training in this very complicated subject both at Montepuez and from the Tanzanians. More importantly, it is testament to the free-wheeling, brainstorming sessions that were common amongst NRA commanders. Encouraging juniors to freely discuss tactical and operational problems with senior commanders was one of the organizational strengths of the rebel army.

After some discussion and modification, Saleh's plan was adopted by the CHC and the assembled commanders. This was on the 15th of January; once the plan was approved, Yoweri Museveni left Masaka to go and brief those commanders who had not been present at the meeting at Masaka Sports Club. First he drove to Hoima by way of Kabamba and Mubende. He spent the night in Hoima and briefed David Tinyefuza (one of the NRA's most senior commanders and presently a four star general in the UPDF). Tinyefuza's mission in the plan was to block the Masindi-Hoima axis against a possible enemy surprise attack originating out of

West-Nile. This attack it was believed would target the rebel army's rear in Fort Portal. Two battalions were placed under Tinyefuza's command: Julius Chihandae's 9th Battalion and Peter Kerim's 19th Battalion.

The following day the CHC drove to Bulamba in Nakaseke district and briefed Ivan Koreta. Koreta's 13th Battalion was based at Bulamba Primary School and was making preparations for their role in the attack. After Bulamba, the CHC drove to Kibibi near Mpigi, where on the evening of the 16th he briefed Matayo Kyaligonza Commanding Officer of the 7th Battalion and his second-in-command Stanley Muhangi. He found 7th Battalion making preparations to attack the enemy position at Kabasanda the following day. 7th Battalion, was to play a pivotal role in the attack on the capital. After briefing Kyaligonza, Museveni returned to Masaka. All this movement on the part of the CHC was in order to preclude the need for radio orders that most likely would have been injurious to the plan's need to attain surprise. The plan required that the enemy be caught wrong footed, that he not expect an attack so soon after Mbarara's capitulation and especially after the signing of the Nairobi Peace Accord.

H-hour as NRA SOPs stipulated, was at 6.35 am on the 17th of January 1986. All units initiated their attacks at that time. 7th battalion attacked and overwhelmed Kabasanda (after a two day fight), then prepared to continue the attack, setting its sights on Mpigi. According to Capt. Ssemakula Godfrey, there was some mis-co-ordination at Kabasanda. Ssemakula was a young fighter in 1st Battalion and subsequently became one of Fred Mugisha's escorts (Mugisha was initially the 2 i/c of 1st Battalion, but from about the time of the battles of River Katonga became the substantive commander). The attack on Kabasanda was supposed to be jointly undertaken by elements of 1st

Battalion and 7th Battalion. There were two enemy positions located on two knolls opposite each other. One was a UNLA post and the other was comprised of ex-Amin soldiers. 1st Battalion attacked the UNLA position and expected 7th Battalion to put in its attack concurrently; but 7th Battalion delayed, and, hence, allowed the ex-Amin elements to re-inforce the fleeing UNLA soldiers and launch a counterattack. 1st Battalion lost a few soldiers in this action. This blunder was blamed on an audacious officer of 7th Battalion called Sam Byaruhanga, who was of Rwandese Tutsi extraction. He was later to die in the Rwandese civil war under unclear circumstances. Nevertheless, the following day Kabasanda fell.

5th Battalion experienced trouble at Kampiringisa about 48 kilometers from Kampala, on the Kampala-Masaka road. Once they were able to put in an attack they overran the enemy force at Kampiringisa. Meanwhile, 7th Battalion attacked Mpigi and overran it.

Once Mpigi fell and was cleared by 7th Battalion, 5th Battalion was able to progress to its blocking position on the Kampala-Entebbe road at Kisubi, to the south of the city. Moving through Nakawuka and Kasanje, Ahmed Kashillingi's 5th Battalion (Steven Kashaka had been re-assigned) occupied its blocking position. After clearing Mpigi, 7th Battalion advanced on the Kampala-Masaka road towards the capital. A force led by Santos Oketcho (a UNLA officer who had recently surrendered to the NRA at Kiboga and had been co-opted) attacked and overwhelmed the UNLA force at Buluba, about 16 kilometers from the capital on the Mityana road. 13th Battalion occupied a blocking position (to prevent enemy reinforcements from reaching the city) opposite Bombo town to the north of the capital.

1st, 3rd and 11th Battalions advanced behind 7th Battalion (actually some of these units were trucked in from Masaka and Katonga), all four battalions had reached the Busega road junction (the entry to the city from the Kampala-Masaka road and Kampala-Mityana road) by the 23rd of January 1986. Meanwhile, the same force that had attacked Buloba utilized the days that it took the other battalions to reach Busega to improve its position, advancing to Lubigi swamp about 4 kilometers from the city.

It had taken 6 days for all units to reach their jumping off points for the final attack on the capital. Saleh ordered the final attack to commence at dawn on the 24th of January 1986.

The CHC had expected a violent struggle at Busega, for two reasons. The natural barrier of the Lubigi swamp provided a defender with excellent opportunities to put up stubborn resistance. Secondly, looking down on this swamp and the road junction was the imposing Mutundwe hill that seemed to be an obvious position for artillery. The leadership of the NRA braced itself for the casualties they were sure would accompany any attack on the Busega road junction. Incredibly, the enemy had established a defensive position at Busega but had left Mutundwe hill unguarded. The NRA wasted no time occupying the hill and converting it into an artillery position. They stationed 14.5mm anti-aircraft guns and mortars there and started pounding the enemy position below them at Busega. The enemy quickly abandoned the critical road junction at Busega.

It was therefore a considerable surprise when word reached the CHC on the morning of the 24th (as he attended a meeting of commanders at Mpigi Town Hall) that the NRA had crossed the Busega road intersection without much of a problem. The enemy had fled. This message was delivered by Saleh who had gotten word from Taban Kyabihende (a company commander in 3rd Battalion). The CHC and Saleh decided to exploit this unexpected good fortune and immediately press the attack. 1st Battalion with 3rd Battalion in support, swept forward and by nightfall had reached Rubaga. These two battalions had been selected to be the main effort (ME) for the attack on the capital. Therefore, the majority of support weapons were issued to these two battle-hardened units. 7th Battalion advanced and by evening had seized Ndeeba. In the fighting for Ndeeba, 7th Battalion lost one of its warriors called Sabatta. 11th Battalion advanced behind 1st and 3rd Battalions and spent that first night in the vicinity of Rubaga.

After receiving word of the rebel army's entry into the capital the CHC moved his command post from Mpigi to the compound of Trinity College Nabbingo (16 kilometers from Kampala on the Kampala-Masaka road). Saleh had reached Nabbingo hours before the CHC and started setting up a tactical operations center (TOC). Yoweri Museveni had intended to hold Salim Saleh close at hand for the duration of the battle. This was so that he might be appraised of the progress of the attack constantly and, consequently, be better able to direct operations; however, events (and Saleh's own restless character) were soon to make this plan unworkable.

The following day (the 25th of January), 3rd Battalion attacked Lubiri and 7th Battalion attacked Makindye. 1st Battalion for now was held back in reserve. The fighting for Lubiri was exceedingly fierce. Sometime in the afternoon of that day an armory around the old Army Shop near Republic House (now called Bulange) was hit by rebel munitions and erupted in a crescendo of explosions. At Nabbingo, Museveni's staff eyed each other nervously (imagining the explosions were the UNLA putting up a ferocious defense of the city).

Finally, Saleh offered to go check on what was going on in the city and Museveni accepted. Saleh set off from Museveni's headquarters at Nabbingo and walked with a few aides to link-up with the fighters in the city. By the time he got to Natete it was already night and it was there he learnt what had caused the explosions earlier in the day. Saleh spent that night at Natete. Republic House fell in the early evening of that day. At Lubiri the enemy fought bravely, the fight went on the whole day; it was not until night fall (about 9.00 pm) that 3rd Battalion was able to seize the garrison. That night one of 3rd Battalion's platoons (commanded by JO II Bruce Muwanga) scaled the wall at Lubiri and discovered that the enemy had fled as soon as it got dark. Meanwhile, 7th Battalion struggled on at Makindye.

The following day (26th of January) with the fighting still raging, Yoweri Museveni, the commander-in-chief of the only rebel army in African history (and one of a handful in world history) to fight a largely autonomous protracted people's war, entered the capital for the first time in five years. He moved his command post to a canteen at the entrance of Republic House which had been captured the day before by 1st and 3rd Battalions. Saleh (who had arrived there earlier) briefed him on the progress of the attack as soon as he entered Republic House.

With the fall of Lubiri the previous day, 1st Battalion was now ordered to seize the heart of the city. Fred Mugisha's 1st Battalion advanced on Bakuli and then onwards through Old Kampala to Kampala road. At Bakuli some companies detached from the battalion and advanced towards Clock Tower by way of Namirembe road, St. Balikudembe Street and finally Queen's Way. The main force pressed on towards Kyaggwe road (where Equatoria Hotel and Kisekka Market currently stand). At Kyaggwe road the fighting was exceedingly intense; 'the bullets were like the sound of a very heavy down pour' recalled President Museveni when the author interviewed him. It was a thunderstorm of automatic fire, a downpour that kills and maims. By midday, 1st Battalion had reached Kampala road. While 1st Battalion fought in the centre of the city, two companies of 3rd Battalion (another two companies had gone to support 1st Battalion's attack) were kneeling in an extended line that stretched from Republic House to Lubiri. They knelt there in echelon facing in the direction of the city, awaiting the order to go to the aid of their brothers in arms. All this time Radio Uganda was still broadcasting, trying to rally the collapsing morale of the defenders. At Parliament Avenue (not far from where Total petrol station and Nandos stand today), the enemy managed to disable one BTR 60 armored personnel carrier (APC) that was supporting 1st Battalion's attack. The NRA had received 3 APCs in the weeks prior to the battle for Kampala as a result of the defection of Major Mande and one lieutenant from the UNLA's fledgeling mechanized forces. The news of this hit briefly rallied the broadcasters at Radio Uganda, who in true UPC fashion started exaggerating this event by reporting that their forces had destroyed a rebel 'tank'.

Captain Ssemakula recalled that the armored vehicle was hit by a rocket launcher, as it reversed to avoid more hits, it ran into a Tata lorry towing a 37mm AAG. The enemy proceeded to burn both weapon systems. This was the cause for the surge in enemy morale that afternoon. However, rallying their men Fred Mugisha and Patrick Lumumba made use of RPGs to silence the enemy's anti-armor entrenchments near Radio Uganda. Ssemakula remembers Mugisha standing erect in the withering fire, urging his men not to retreat. Such boldness roused the men and they counter-attacked driving the enemy back.

By 3.00 pm Radio Uganda had been secured. 11th Battalion had also achieved its objectives advancing through Nakulabye, Makerere, Kamwokya and attacking Summit View by the afternoon of the 26th. 11th Battalion managed to overran Summit View and drive out a large number of enemy soldiers under the command of LTC. Eric Odwar. Prior to this, 11th Battalion had heard that 1st Battalion had experienced some difficulties around Radio Uganda. They quickly dispatched a force to come to the aid of 1st Battalion (and also to be the ones to capture Radio Uganda). Ssemakula recalled that this force linked up with them around where the Garden City/Oasis Mall roundabout currently is located. *'Mbio eli kuwa sio mbio'* in Ssemakula's words, meaning, 11th Battalion reinforcements were running at full tilt. So, understandably they were disappointed to see that 1st Battalion had already captured the much coveted Radio Uganda.

The fight for Makindye raged on, causing some unease amongst the NRA fighters. While the CHC waited for a resolution of the fight at Makindye barracks, a sweating Julius Aine (a company commander of 5th Battalion) appeared at Republic House. He related to Saleh how a large enemy force had broken through 5th Battalion's blocking position at Kisubi. Aine had run from Kisubi to Republic House to inform his superiors about the incident on Entebbe road. Apparently, Kashillingi had deployed only half of 5th Battalion (Julius Aine's and China Mafundo's companies) to block the enemy and had kept the other half some distance away (essentially splitting his force). An enemy force of approximately 1,000 (from Entebbe) had little difficulty brushing aside Kashillingi's reduced force on the road. In the words of Yoweri Museveni, in his autobiography, 'This was a worrying moment because we really did not have enough forces to counter this attack'[49]. Confronted with this threat and recognizing the potential for it to seriously complicate the whole attack, the CHC dispatched Saleh and the two companies of 3rd Battalion (that were still close at hand) to deal with this enemy force. Saleh, Lumumba, Aine and the two companies ran from Republic House in the direction of Entebbe road. This left the CHC with no tactical reserve and was the cause of his 'worrying' that afternoon and evening. 1st Battalion was still engaging the enemy towards Jinja road, 11th Battalion was clearing Kololo of enemy forces and 7th Battalion was still fighting at Makindye (clearly the longest action of the entire attack).

Jet's Special Force was stopped from occupying a blocking position at Jinja road (by an order from Saleh) with the effect that enemy units started fleeing the capital by that route. The Special Force was redirected to aid Ivan Koreta's 13th Battalion on Gulu road (to the north of the city) and became embroiled in fighting on that sector. They eventually managed to fight their way to Kawempe by which time the enemy had culminated (given up).

Saleh advanced with 3rd Battalion, ensuring that he remained in radio contact with the CHC; they took up positions at Namasuba (which is the valley just beyond Najjankumbi hill if you're facing Entebbe). They were facing south. Meanwhile, one of Kashillingi's companies (one of those that had not been deployed on the road to block the enemy) had raced on the western side of Entebbe road and linked up with the two companies of 3rd Battalion at Namasuba. 3rd Battalion's two companies were commanded by JO I Levi Karuhanga (now a Major General in the UPDF) and JO I Taban Kyabihende (now a Brigadier in the UPDF). Colonel Kavuma, (who was now a Provisional JO II and commanding one platoon in Karuhanga's company) remembered that the companies stretched out on either side of the road in an extended line.

The enemy force from Entebbe entered the valley (as it grew dark) and was given a bloody nose; they fell back in the dark. Saleh had positioned himself at the UEB offices at Najjanankumbi overlooking the valley. Tragically, JO II Rwabwisho (the hero of the rear guard action at Kembogo) was killed in this clash. The NRA units surged forward and occupied Zana hill. The enemy got wind that another force to their rear was closing in on them (this was China Mafundo's company that had remained behind at Kisubi when Aine's was dispersed). Sensing that they were about to be caught in a pincer movement, the enemy sent an emissary to indicate their willingness to surrender. Saleh, who arrived at Zana just as the emissary was being received, immediately accepted their surrender and the entire force of 1,000 soldiers capitulated.

In the early evening of the 26th of January, 7th Battalion finally conquered Makindye and thus became available as a reserve. This was before the situation at Namasuba had been resolved. The CHC re-deployed 7th Battalion to Kibuye round-about, facing Entebbe and thus had extra forces in case 3rd Battalion was overwhelmed. At about 10.00 pm, Saleh radioed to inform Museveni that the entire enemy force of 1000 had surrendered. Saleh's words were '*Afande tumemaliza!*' ('Sir, we have finished' or more poetically 'mission accomplished'). This radio message signaled the end of the Ugandan resistance war.

At some point that evening as the situation on Entebbe road continued to pre-occupy Yoweri Museveni's mind, one Brigadier Lowles (commander of the British Military Assistance Training Team or 'BMATT' that was training the UNLA) was presented to the CIIC. NRA units had come across him in the course of the battle. Apparently, he was agitated that NRA commanders had ignored his demands for them to escort some people around the battlefield. Uncomprehending of this Brit (and really not impressed by him), the NRA commanders had sent him to the CHC to get him out of their hair. Brigadier Lowles knew that he was dealing with a different bunch of people, when Museveni told him in no uncertain terms, that his commanders were in the middle of a war and had other exigencies to keep them busy. Soon after the fall of Kampala, both Brigadier Lowles and the British High Commissioner at the time were re-called to London by a furious Thatcher administration. Apparently, the two men had been spinning the story that the NRA would never seize power in Uganda and that the UNLA was very strong. The 'Iron Lady' had every right to be indignant at these two individuals and their poor analysis of the prospects for victory of the Ugandan resistance.

Ssemakula remembered that Akanga Byaruhanga came to see them (1st Battalion) at Radio Uganda (where Mugisha established his CP) that evening in a white pick-up. He relayed a message from the CHC, 'they had done very well!' An exhausted Saleh returned to the city after the events at Namasuba and Zana, he joined 1st Battalion at Radio Uganda and collapsed in a heap in the compound. It had been five days since he had last gotten any sleep.

After the battle Ssemakula managed to get a pair of shoes from the UNLA's logistics stocks around the city. He had fought for a total of 2 years and four months (he had joined the resistance in September of 1983) without shoes.

Analysis

The dissimilarities between the sieges of Masaka and Mbarara and the battle for Kampala are stark. At both Masaka and Mbarara, the war had evolved into a contest of wills between the belligerents, before the garrisons had been slowly asphyxiated by the imposition of two relentless blockades. At Kampala, the enemy was overpowered by superior conventional power and by direct assault. The reasons for this as has already been described were the enlargement of the NRA's battalions and the arms build up that occurred prior to the battle. This point is demonstrated by the fact that it took two days to capture the capital city, as contrasted with the 3 months it took to seize two provincial capitals. However, the more subtle yet potent point is that the UNLA's morale (that critical intangible of war) had been devastated; this had been achieved at the decisive battle of Kembogo. At Kembogo, the UNLA's operational COG had been smashed by Mobile Brigade and the psychological effects of that crushing defeat were still resonating at the battle of Kampala. A 'defeat phenomenon' had been imposed on the UNLA and they no longer had much stomach for a fight.

Saleh's plan for the attack on Kampala exhibited a military professionalism that was not proportionate with the limited (if that) training in urban operations, he had received in Mozambique or at Jinja (from the Tanzanians). The training of the Montepuez cadre had been based on extensive and practical knowledge in weapons training. They all had to undergo intensive training on five weapon types: pistols; kalashnikovs; carbines; machine guns and RPGs. After this, each one of them was required to specialize in either mines or mortars. There was a component of urban operations training, but not one that could be described as extensive and thorough.

Saleh's plan for the attack on Kampala was indicative of the very accurate maxim that 'necessity is the mother of invention'. The minds of the rebel commanders had been concentrated in the crucible of a protracted people's war and this had served as the ideal military academy, complete with field training exercises (FTXs) that endured for years and with live fire exercises. They had learnt many valuable lessons in this 'house of war'. Additionally, the NRA was a 'learning organization' where hierarchy was respected but not deified. Indeed, leaders who were inflexible or unwilling to interact with their subordinates were censured and identified as problematic. Good leaders were recognized as those who were pro-active, soliciting ideas and solutions from their juniors. Saleh represented this genre of commander, always self-effacing and eager to hear (and often implement) the views of those he led. A major reason for this flat organizational (networked) culture was the NRA's genesis as a guerrilla outfit.

The NRA had begun as a collection of sections, platoons and companies dispersed over thousands of square kilometers in the Luwero Triangle. These small and dispersed units were largely autonomous. Therefore, they could only be guided by a commander's intent. This commander's intent exhorted them to attack the enemy on the move (i.e. avoid attacking the enemy in entrenched positions), avoid battles of long duration, seek out soft targets, attack the enemy's means for making war (mainly economic targets), avoid holding ground and above all preserve and expand friendly forces while wearing down the enemy's forces. Some of these precepts could be described as comprising part of the NRA's 'doctrine' (something that will be handled in greater scope in chapter 12). The commander's intent, told them what to do (the tactical principles of the war they were fighting) not how to do it; it, therefore, facilitated initiative and imagination. The German concept of 'Auftragstaktik' or mission type tactics were at the core of the NRA's style of command and execution. 'The concept of Auftragstaktik or "mission tactics" ... made it the responsibility of each German officer and NCO ... to do without question or doubt whatever the situation required, as he personally saw it. Omission and inactivity were considered worse than a wrong choice of expedient. Even disobedience of orders was not inconsistent with this philosophy'[50].

The UNLA's plan for the defense of Kampala revealed a fundamental lack of understanding for operations in built up areas (OBUA). Bazilio's UNLA could have easily turned Kampala into a very costly and prolonged battle had they adhered to the precepts of defensive operations in urban terrain. These principles of defensive operations in urban areas, instruct the defender to utilize small teams of infantry bearing machine-guns, sniper rifles and anti-tank weaponry to disrupt and channel the attacker into well prepared ambushes. Buildings are turned into strongpoints which are mutually supporting, streets and roads are blocked and local counter-attacks furnished by the presence of reserves. It is an aggressive defense, as even a cursory study of urban warfare would have demonstrated to the UNLA commanders. However, they had no time for study, showing more flair for terrorizing 'Kampalans' and for drinking at Nile Mansions. It should, therefore, come as no surprise that Nile Mansions was selected as the headquarters for the UNLA's defense of Kampala. This is the place Bazilio Okello (the UNLA's Chief of Defense Forces) situated himself and the cream of the UNLA hierarchy. Their plan for the defense of the city was abysmal.

It was not until D+6 that all participating rebel battalions were in position, at their alloted jumping off points for the attack on the capitial. Unlike other units, 7th Battalion had to seize Mpigi (a middle-sized town) before advancing to participate in the battle for Kampala. 5th Battalion (which experienced its own difficulties at Kampiringisa) could not initiate its advance towards the Kampala-Entebbe road until 7th Battalion was through fighting for Mpigi. Once all the units were in position, the assault on the capital was initiated on the 24th of January 1986 (D+7).

By this time the investment of the capital seemed to have been achieved, except for Jinja road. The break-in battle (by the 4 battalions: 1st, 3rd, 7th and 11th) was swift and relatively effortless because the UNLA failed to create a perimeter force to protect the approaches to the capital. The critical road junction at Busega, was defended in an appalling fashion. Both Mutundwe hill and the Lubigi swamp were left without defenders. Once the break-in battalions penetrated the outskirts of the city (without much opposition) they moved rapidly to secure objectives, attacking the main garrisons the following day. The enemy garrisons put up a stiff resistance and particularly so at Makindye. Makindye was located in close terrain, with a lot of shabby outbuildings surrounding it. The enemy occupied these buildings and additionally set up machine gun pillboxes on the road junctions leading up to the garrison. The fighting to take these defended buildings and pillboxes developed into a bitter one. Whoever was charged with the defense of Makindye had some understanding of defensive operations in built up areas; his deployment is witness to this fact. 7th Battalion had a tougher nut to crack because of these correct defensive measures. It took the better part of two days for Makindye to fall.

By 9.00 pm on the 25th of January, Lubiri (the largest garrison in the capital) had fallen to 3rd Battalion. On the 26th of January, 1st Battalion moved to secure the city center, capturing Radio Uganda by 3.00 pm that day. 11th Battalion that had advanced by way of Nakulabye, finally managed to secure its last objective (Kololo Summit View) at around the same time (3.00 pm). Meanwhile, 7th Battalion's battle at Makindye raged on. Makindye only fell at dusk on that day.

Then as so often happens in war, just as the attack seemed to be about to produce the results that the rebel army had dreamt of for so long, 'Murphy's law' started taking effect. 5th Battalion which was supposed to block the Kampala-Entebbe road at Kisubi was scattered by a force of some 1000 enemy soldiers. This was caused by an error in deployment committed by 5th Battalion's commander. Now with 3 battalions immersed in the fighting, the CHC had to commit his only reserve (two companies of 3rd Battalion) to the emergency on Entebbe road. Along with this reserve, the CHC sent two of his most competent commanders: Salim Saleh and Patrick Lumumba. These two men's feats in the war of resistance were by now legendary. While most would tremble at the prospect of losing their lives so late in the war and with victory so tantalizingly close, these two remarkable men thought nothing of plunging once again into the 'realm of danger, chance and uncertainity'.

However, along with the derring-do of heroes like Saleh, Kyaligonza, Lumumba, Rwigema, Mugisha, Muhangi, Pecos, Jet, Tinyefuza, Chefe Ali, Bruce Muwanga, Sabatta and Rwabwisho were the quiet acts of daily courage of young fighters like Ssemakula; these were utterly selfless and committed soldiers who unflinchingly bore the brunt of the fighting and suffering. Along with the unimaginable hardships, Ssemakula remembers light moments. Kabuura (one of the CHC's longstanding escorts), for instance, would lightheartedly ask him in Swahili (which he was still not good at) *'Oko mwana ume ama mwana mke?'* Meaning 'are you a man or woman?' To which he would falteringly answer, *'Niko mwana mke'* ('I'm a woman'), Ssemakula humorously recalled when the author interviewed him. Also, he would hear fighters preparing to go for 'recce' (reconnaissance) and think they were going to the 'lake'. 'What lake are these people constantly going to?' He would ask himself.

After the action at Namasuba, 5th Battalion with one platoon from 3rd Battalion advanced and liberated Entebbe. The platoon from 3rd Battalion chosen for this purpose was none other than Kavuma's. Entebbe was cleared with little difficulty and Kavuma's platoon was detailed to guard State House (the old State House that was demolished in 2004 before the current and inifinitely more imposing one was built). Col. Kavuma recalled that on entering State House, the immaculate staff offered him (this conquering bushman from Luwero) a bed to sleep on. 'It had the whitest sheets I had ever seen', a laughing Kavuma recalled when I interviewed him. 'I knew then that for me at least the war was finally over', he continued with a cheeky wink.

The battle for Kampala was the culmination of the Ugandan resistance war, in Clausewitzian speak [it was the tactical engagement that directly achieved the political object of the war]. Kampala had to be taken in order for the war to have met the purposes for which it was launched in the first place; it had to be taken in order for the Ugandan revolution to achieve an outright military triumph. Kampala was not only the grand finale of the struggle, it was also the biggest battle the rebel army had fought up to that point. It involved an attack by a division sized force against approximately 12,000 defenders. In keeping with the maneuverist theme of the war of resistance, casualties on both sides were light with the NRA suffering about 20 dead to the UNLA's 80 killed in action. However, these light casualties could not mask the fact that the UNLA was a shattered force and as proof nearly 3,000 UNLA soldiers were captured or surrendered in Kampala. The remaining 9,000 defenders and their families all fled the city.

The goal of the resistance had always been the overthrow of the dictatorships; this, it was recognized, could only be done by an armed revolution utilizing a people's war strategy. Mao's theory of a people's war stipulated that the military instrument was only one of a number of tools (the others being of a political, social and economic nature) that in combination would overcome the initial weaknesses of the revolutionary authority vis a vis the reactionary power. However, in both China's and Uganda's experience the final blow was dealt by the military instrument within people's war. The Ugandan resistance war was undoubtedly predominantly a military affair. Writing in March 1985, Yoweri Museveni exposed the failure of the other instruments within people's war to make any impact on the Ugandan situation:

> 'Chiefly because of the weaknesses of our external workers, it was not possible to get material assistance from outside. A number of good projects were ruined by so called high-ranking officials on our External Committee. In spite of this, however the internal wing has been able to sustain the struggle and expand it with quite a lot of hardships which should and could have been avoided. Our civilian supporters have been subjected to severe repression that would have been prevented if we had received external assistance'[51].

'The internal wing' was the military tool (the NRA) and the heroic battles it fought from 1981-1986. Like China and Cuba, the Ugandan revolution was purchased chiefly by battlefield successes. None more so, than the climactic battle for Kampala, where the UNLA finally lost its hold on political power.

What could have been done differently? The change in orders for Jet's Special Force permitted badly mauled enemy units to escape. Saying that presents a bit of a quandary to the analyst, for the failure to close the gap at Jinja road was both a setback and a blessing. Had the enemy surmised that there was no escape from the battle, the fighting might have gotten a lot more fierce; however, the fact that a considerable number of units escaped ensured that the counter-revolution (that was launched 8 months after the victory at Kampala) would not be lacking in military strength (at least initially). Additionally, the escaping enemy vented his wrath on the towns and villages that lay in his path. According to Ondoga ori Amaza, the UNLA '...on 29 January 1986 rampaged in the eastern town of Mbale, killing up to 50 civilians in addition to looting the town'[52]. It is uncertain whether the Special Force (a force of about 500 men) could have completely blocked Jinja road, nor would have this been necessarily desirable. Nevertheless, the Special Force might have set an ambush along this route ensuring that a significant number of enemy units did not make it out of the city, or at least that the retreating enemy's integrity was disrupted.

In ordering Jet not to seal off the Jinja road exit from the city, Saleh and indeed the other commanders involved in the fight were cognizant of the fact that they were virtually guaranteeing a rematch between the NRA and its armed opposition. However, the leaders had determined not to cause unnecessary loss of life especially to the retreating enemy's dependants. For the UNLA retreated lock, stock and barrel taking their families with them. In the words of Saleh, 'We knew it would be a blood bath and their families would perish in the fighting, so we decided to give them an escape route'. 'It was really for humanitarian reasons that we let them escape', Saleh continued when the author interviewed him. The CHC was briefed on this collective reasoning and approved. For the victorious commander of a revolutionary force that had suffered incomparably for five years in a brutal people's war to be thinking of the 'humanitarian' condition of his enemy (who had caused all this enormous pain in the first place) reveals the high sensibilities and refined intelligence of Salim Saleh.

Conclusion

This minor glitch (the inability to close Jinja road) does not take away from the remarkable success that the battle for Kampala represented. It was the climactic battle of a people's war without rival on the African continent. It was the first time in African history that a revolutionary and popular force that had been nurtured in the hinterlands was forcefully taking political power (by military action) in the capital of a nation. For even in the great liberation movements in southern Africa (Mozambique, Angola, Zimbabwe, Namibia), in Guinea-Bissau and Algeria the revolutionaries had seized power by way of a collapse in the political will and morale of the oppressors. In Uganda, for the first time in Africa revolutionaries had won an outright military victory. Yoweri Museveni had started out by trying to emulate the experiences in southern Africa (especially Mozambique) but had achieved a great deal more; he had in effect transformed the African experience in waging people's war.

Indeed, what the NRA achieved was no less than the undiluted and unadulterated fulfillment of Mao's theory of people's war, all this with little foreign help. It was beyond doubt a herculean achievement. The battle of Kampala was conducted with a professionalism and speed that even at the time impressed all. I remember as a young boy watching the battle hardened and bedraggled NRA columns, marching triumphantly through the streets of Kampala, on the nightly news in Sweden. It was impossible not to feel a tremendous surge of national pride at what our great compatriots had achieved. The Ugandan people had 'stood up'! They had by their own efforts defied history and an uncaring international community; they had liberated themselves.

Notes

48. Pecos Kutesa, *Uganda's Revolution 1979-1986*, How I Saw It (Fountain Publishers Ltd, Kampala, 2008) 210
49. Yoweri Museveni, *Sowing the Mustard Seed*, (Malaysia, Macmillan Publishers Limited, 2007) 174.
50. Auftragstaktik, http://www.ducimus.com/Archive/auftrags-oleary.htm (accessed 25 November, 2009)
51.. Lt.Gen. Yoweri Kaguta Museveni, Three Essays on Military Strategy in Uganda ( ) 31
52. Ondoga ori Amaza, *Museveni's Long March*, From Guerrilla to Statesman (Fountain Publishers Ltd, Kampala, 1998) 114

Picture Section B

NRA fighters in the bush

NRA guerrillas marching in Luwero

Museveni addressing NRA fighters in Luwero

NRA officers in the bush; Gen. Elly Tumwiine (first right) followed by Fred Rwigema

Battles of the Ugandan Resistance: A Tradition of Maneuver   185

Top commanders of UNLA: Generals Oyite Ojok and Bazilio Okello

NRA fighters: Patrick Lumumba and James Kazini

Rwigema and NRA fighters triumphantly enter one of the towns in western Uganda

Saleh's command post in Masaka

NRA fighters taking over Kampala

Yoweri Museveni swearing in as president of Uganda, 29 January 1986

NRA combatants arrive at Nimule in West Nile to mark the complete liberation of the country

General Yoweri Museveni as Commander in Chief of the UPDF

Battles of the Ugandan Resistance: A Tradition of Maneuver   189

The author during his training at the US Army's Airborne School in Fort Benning, Georgia

The author at the Command and General Staff College in Fort Leavenworth Kansas, USA

The author (foreground) motivating the troops

The author (3rd from left) during Operation Lightning Thunder in DRC

11

What Was the Strategy of the Resistance War?

> *'Strategy without tactics is the slowest route to victory. Tactics without strategy is the noise before defeat.'*
>
> Sun Tzu

This is a question that has intrigued me for some time now. Did the 27 armed men who attacked Kabamba on the 6th of February consciously adhere to a strategy? Or were they simply more adept (than the enemy) at altering their methods to a mutating war situation? No doubt the more doctrinaire leaders of the resistance will claim that they had prescient knowledge of events and that things went more or less according to plan. However, others within the upper crust of the resistance leadership are more humble and guarded about the way things turned out.

What is strategy? For the answer, we must once again turn our attention (not for the first time in this book) to the instruction of the master Carl von Clausewitz. For Clausewitz, 'strategy' represented the link between military power and the political goals for which that force is required. 'Strategy', Clausewitz said, 'Is the use of engagements for the object of the war'[53]. Clausewitz, as always, was concerned with the 'real conditions' of war; what he called the 'grammar' of war. The difficulty (in his opinion) was how to link the dirty and messy business of tactical engagements with the higher realms of strategy. He saw a clear relationship between the tactical level of war (where engagements are fought) and the political purposes of the war. 'War', the great Prussian said, 'is nothing but the continuation of policy with other means'[54]. Policy (or politics) is what gives war and strategy their purpose; otherwise in Clausewitz's opinion war would be pointless. The instrumentality of war was central to Clausewitz's understanding of both war and strategy (at least military strategy).

This view has elicited some criticism from a number of modern military historians, like John Keegan, who argue that Clausewitz's view is too dependent on the model of the Westphalian state system*. That is to say that Clausewitz's definition of strategy and war resonates with the idea of sovereign nation states pursuing national interests (or policies) in an international system where all states are equal, have right of political self-determination and are protected from the intervention of other states in their internal affairs. For people like John Keegan this definition is too narrow; war pre-dates the Westphalian state system; war is part of the condition of man. The link between the two points of view (Clausewitz's and Keegan's) has to do with

---

* The Westphalian system is a concept of international relations based on certain core ideas: sovereignty of states; equality between states; and non-intervention of one state into the domestic affairs of another. This understanding of international relations emerged with the Peace of Westphalia (1648), in which major European countries agreed to respect each others territorial integrity. The Peace of Westphalia is commonly understood to represent the beginning of modern international relations.

the idea of 'policy'. Whose policy? National policy or the policy of an autocratic monarch?

Although it is certainly true that war precedes the Peace of Westphalia of 1648 and the rise of modern nation states (starting with the French Revolution in 1789), it is not immediately clear how this presents a contradiction with Clausewitz's view that 'war is a continuation of policy with other means'. It is true that national policy, as we know it today, was birthed with the overthrow of absolute monarchs; the key event was the French Revolution (1789). Policy ceased to be the preserve of an absolute ruler, exercising this prerogative through a privy council and became the corporate property of the nation. Therefore, authentic 'politics' (i.e. the competition to manage society) only emerged with the French Revolution. Only then could the inhabitants of the monarch's realm 'own' political power (through representatives) and, therefore, have impact on a particular community's choices and priorities. Therefore, although it is certainly true that Clausewitz's definition reverberates more with the post-1789 world (he was after all fixated on Napoleon Bonaparte), it is important to observe that even absolute monarch's pursued policies. True, these were often whimsical and undemocratic; but it was policy nonetheless.

The critical ingredient it seems for 'war' to be 'war', is that it must be organized violence and must serve some policy goal (national or other). This is what distinguishes war from other forms of conflict, e.g. tenants spontaneously lynching landlords over threatened evictions, as is the case presently with the tensions and conflicts over land legislation in Uganda. Of course, one could argue (as did the French revolutionaries) that absolute monarchs have no legitimacy at all and, therefore, cannot formulate any policy worthy of the name. Being a republican creature myself, I am positively sympathetic to this viewpoint; but this may not be the case for the humble subject of a monarch, conditioned from infancy to be in awe of his god-like prince.

Clausewitz explained that, 'Everything in strategy is very simple, but that does not make everything easy'[55]. The reason for this difficulty in pursuing strategy (according to Clausewitz) is that unlike tactical situations where decisions are made based upon the exigencies of the moment (i.e. the grammar of war), in strategy the picture is rarely clear. Everything in strategy takes time, so one is not immediately aware whether one's decisions are correct or are having the desired effect. The accomplished strategist must, therefore, be an individual of supreme patience and self-assurance. For before the saplings of the desired outcome emerge, ones strategic choices will endure countless tribulations. It is probably for this reason that Yoweri Museveni's autobiography took its name from the Biblical parable of the mustard seed. For his 'strategy' had been buffeted by innumerable trials (or 'diversions' as Clausewitz would say), just like that mustard seed had to overcome initial disadvantages before becoming the largest tree in the garden.

For many a strategist, it seems they are pregnant with an idea whose time has not come but they must hold fast and keep the faith. For Yoweri Museveni, this idea was that the Ugandan people could be rallied and led to overthrow the dictatorships of Amin and Obote. More astoundingly, Museveni's idea proposed that the Ugandan people could achieve this by their own efforts. For the majority of the intelligentsia in Uganda in the 1970s and 1980s, he might as well have been speaking Martian.

In 1981 (at the start of the resistance war) Museveni laid out his thinking on the strategy of the war. In this emotionally charged document (no doubt heavily influenced by the tactical pressures and real dangers of a guerrilla campaign) titled 'Why we fought a Protracted People's War', Museveni explains his understanding of strategy. He says, 'Strategy means the methodology one uses to solve a problem as a whole, that is, to solve a problem from A to Z. Tactics on the other hand, are the methods one uses to solve parts of a problem from A to B or from B to C'[56]. In this definition of strategy, Museveni showed an understanding for the broadness of strategy. He appreciated that strategy is composed of a number of dimensions, of which the military tool is but one component. Museveni's understanding of tactics focused on the military instrument. This has some similarities to Clausewitz's understanding of strategy except for one important difference: Clausewitz limited his analysis to the nexus between strategy and the military tool; in other words, he did not consider the other dimensions of strategy. Clausewitz's understanding of strategy had applicability in the strictly military dimension.

Museveni's understanding of strategy must be understood in the light of the Maoist philosophy that profoundly influenced him. Mao's understanding of strategy was shaped by the gruelling circumstances of the life and death struggle he engaged in with the Chinese Nationalists, led by Chiang Kai Shek and later with the Japanese. Confronted with the immense military superiority of his enemies, Mao perceived the political nature of warfare; war to him was not just the clash of armies; it was a life and death struggle that pitted every strength that the belligerents possessed against each other. Warfare was, therefore, broader than a reliance on the military instrument alone.

In this struggle, Mao intended to fully exploit the entire spectrum of societal forces to bring about the collapse of his enemies. He saw no delineation between politics and military tasks, in fact the People's Liberation Army (PLA) was supposed to be in the vanguard of implementing the Communist Party's political program. For Mao, war was 'politics with bloodshed'[57]. He said, 'The Red Army fights not merely for the sake of fighting but in order to conduct propaganda among the masses, organize them, arm them, and help them to establish revolutionary political power. Without these objectives, fighting loses its meaning and the Red Army loses the reason for its existence'[58].

Mao's 'people's war strategy' sought to move the revolutionaries from a situation of being on the 'strategic defense' to one of launching a 'strategic counteroffensive'. Mao (ever the consummate realist) did not have reliable allies in his fight with the Nationalists and Japanese; he realized that it would take a lot of time to win the war. However, he was quick to make the long time lines inherent in a people's war work for him. He turned time into a weapon. Mao did the same with geography, utilizing China's difficult terrain to negate the advantages of his enemy's superior firepower. His pre-occupation was with preserving the morale of his forces through battlefield victories, at every stage of his people's war strategy (i.e. guerrilla warfare, mobile warfare and conventional warfare). Mao recognized that in spite of his military inferiority in relation to his enemies, it was still possible to use China's vast land mass and even greater population to achieve combat superiority at the point of decision. In Mao's mind, the Chinese Communists could fight battles of encirclement and decision at the tactical/operational level while simultaneously being on the strategic defensive and fighting a protracted war. This all gelled in with Mao's stated 'object of the war' which was to 'to preserve oneself and destroy the enemy'[59].

Mao understood that strategy contained a number of 'dimensions'; these dimensions included elements like politics, culture, people, economics, technology, geography, time and military operations. All these dimensions had a bearing on achieving success in any strategy. It was the responsibility of the strategist to weld all these different but connected constituents of strategy and generate successes. This is the reason why limiting oneself to the military facet alone (within strategy), was antithetical to Mao's understanding of strategy. The accomplished strategist would orchestrate all these dimensions and use them to exert influence on the target until the desired outcome was realized.

However, there can be no doubt that Mao perceived an outright military victory as the natural and intended goal of a people's war strategy. Indeed, the other dimensions within strategy played a secondary and complementary role to the military instrument. Later practitioners were to discover that if properly executed, people's war strategy can lead to a collapse of the enemy long before the military instrument has developed adequate strength to deliver the coup de grace. This for example, was the case with the Sandinista Revolution in Nicaragua in 1979.

This holistic view of strategy was different from Clausewitz's purely military understanding of strategy, i.e. as 'the use of engagements for the object of the war'. Colin S. Gray, has referred to these dimensions as 'distinctive points of view of a single complex phenomenon than as discrete subjects - the whole house of strategy'[60]. Much like a house is composed of different structural elements – the foundation, walls, ceiling, internal compartments, staircases etc - each distinct, yet combining with the rest to form a complete unit; thus the different constituents of strategy merge to produce a well-defined strategic experience.

It is this complex and nuanced understanding that informed Mao's grasp of strategy. People's war is infused with this conception of strategy. It is pretty certain that this was Museveni's understanding of strategy*. He had reverently studied Mao throughout the 1970s in Tanzania and absorbed his writings with the fervour of a man seeking revolutionary redemption. Whenever he was racked by doubt, he would return to the orthodoxy of Maoist thought. Additionally, Museveni read British and Canadian field manuals surreptitiously given to him by one of the TPDF's most revolutionary and dynamic officers called Colonel Ali Mafudh. Ali Mafudh was of Zanzibari origin, he was also an avowed pan-Africanist. He had helped restore order in Zanzibar after the assasination of Sheikh Abeid Karume, the first President of Zanzibar. Colonel Ali Mafudh rose to become the TPDF's Chief of Operations and Training (COT) and it was in this capacity that he quenched Museveni's thirst for military pamphlets.

There were remarkable similarities in the circumstances of Museveni and Mao Zedong. When Mao in his writings talks of the backwardness of Chinese society, her military inferiority in comparison with her enemies, her semi-colonized status, the privations of her rural population and her isolation in the face of overwhelming challenges in the 1930s, he might as well have been writing about Uganda in the early 1980s. So it was patently obvious to Museveni that of all the theorists of war and strategy, Mao was the most compelling and relevant.

Mao spoke of attaining a favourable 'correlation of forces' before the revolutionaries could launch their strategic counter-offensive. By

---

*   Museveni had never read Clausewitz's masterpiece, *On War*.

this he meant that when most of the dimensions of strategy were stacked in favour of his side, it would be appropriate to throttle his enemies. In much the same sense, Museveni spoke of 'balance of forces' in his 1981 tract (that was mentioned above); he wrote: 'When the balance of forces has shifted in our favour, we shall launch conventional warfare. This entails fighting positional warfare for control of towns and strategic points'[61].

For both Mao and Museveni, it was only through the adept wielding of these elements of strategy that victory would be achieved. Ironically, in the Ugandan experience it was the military dimension in the form of the matchless National Resistance Army that assured the sustenance of the revolution and final victory. The resolute support of the people of Luwero, Ngoma, Singo and Bulemezi in general has to be understood in the context of their inextricable ties to the NRA. Their support was for the fighters whom they lived with and daily saw meting out punishments on the dictatorship for the unspeakable atrocities committed against them. It was an empirical relationship based on the numerous struggles they had jointly endured. Had the NRA been a talking shop, simply carrying out propaganda and political classes, there is little doubt that it would have soon lost all credibility with the people. Successful armed action was a necessity for the support of the peasants in the Luwero Triangle and in the west of the country. The two measures had to go hand in hand, but military success was critical.

Museveni's obvious disappointment in the External Committee reveals that the other dimensions (e.g. diplomatic efforts to procure arms from external sponsors) were not working out at all, yet this was more than compensated for by the brilliance of the NRA and its battlefield successes. Hence, starting out with a Maoist conception of strategy, the NRA's practice of strategy mutated (in the heat or 'grammar' of the resistance war) into something akin to Clausewitz's understanding of strategy.

This brilliance of the NRA's commanders led by Museveni, was a consequence of a pragmatic approach to the challenges of the war. In this regard, these practical men devised solutions after a careful process of observation, orientation and decision-making. Once the decision was taken, action based on those decisions would follow and so incrementally tactical changes were implemented that bore strategic fruit. This system that was christened the 'OODA loop' (for Observation-Orientation-Decision-Action) or 'Boyd's cycle' after Colonel John Boyd of the U.S. Airforce, who first described it after the Korean war (where United States airmen flying F-86 Sabre jets, had achieved favourable kill ratios in dogfights against North Korean Mig-15s), had definite applicability in the Ugandan resistance war. War is a Darwinian environment, either you adapt and survive or the grammar of war will annihilate you. It really is survival for the fittest in war. Therefore, without knowing it, the tactical excellence of the NRA had transformed the strategy of the war from the Maoist model into a Clausewitzian template. Colin S. Gray's words that 'Strategy is as difficult to perform well in a purposive manner as it is all too rarely performed consciously at all'[62] resonate powerfully with the reality of the resistance war.

If we can digress for a moment, from this discussion the question arises: 'can we decode a distinctly Ugandan strategic culture?' Strategic preferences are influenced by cultural context, strategy is not beyond culture. In the military (or security) context, culture can be understood as '[comprising] the persisting socially transmitted ideas, attitudes, traditions, habits of mind, and preferred methods of operation that are more or less specific to a particular geographically based security community that has had unique historical experience'[63]. Strategic culture, therefore, relates to the prefered *modus operandi* and habits of mind that a particular security community favours. The strategic culture of Germans in the pre-World War II years and that of the British were clearly different. The Germans influenced by the reality of vulnerable land borders (and powerful rivals in the east and west) were biased towards land operations; whereas, the British perceived that their security and commercial interests were best served by enhancing their maritime power.

In the same sense, does our maneuverist history offer us a cultural frame of reference? This is an interesting question and certainly should be explored further. It is certain that we shall discover that in relation to our brother states in the East African Community, certain distinct cultural patterns will start to emerge. For example, we may find that Kenya and Tanzania have a cultural proclivity for maritime operations and Uganda and Rwanda are the exemplar of maneuver on land. Even within these categories certain sub-cultures arise, for example, the military culture of an aviator and an infantry grunt (both components of land operations) are vastly different. This differentiation would obviously support the rationalization of our collective military capabilities, assigning to each state a role that it is historically and culturally competent to perform.

Thus in the final analysis, it was battles that decided the issue in the Ugandan resistance war. The people, politics, time, economics and technology all had contributory effect (especially the people and time); but it was military operations that achieved the 'object of the war'. 'Maneuver warfare', a core idea within people's war, typified the struggle. The strategic object of the war came to be purchased by the battlefield successes of the NRA, the primacy of combat had been borne out by events. Clausewitz's dictum that 'The decision of arms is for all major and minor operations in war what cash payment is in commerce. Regardless how complex the relationship between the two parties, regardless how rarely settlements actually occur, they can never be entirely absent...'[64] had held true in the Ugandan experience.

Notes

53. Carl von Clausewitz, *On War*, (New York, Princeton University Press, 1993), 146
54. Carl von Clausewitz, *On War*, (New York, Princeton University Press, 1993), 77
55. Carl von Clausewitz, *On War*, (New York, Princeton University Press, 1993), 209
56. Lt.Gen. Yoweri Kaguta Museveni, *Three Essays on Military Strategy in Uganda* ( ) 7
57. Mao Zedong, *On Protracted War*,
58. Peter Paret, *Makers of Modern Strategy*, (New Jersey, Princeton University Press,1986), 840
59. Mao Zedong, *On Protracted War*,
60. Colin S. Gray, *Modern Strategy*, (Oxford, Oxford University Press, 1999), 22
61. Lt.Gen. Yoweri Kaguta Museveni, *Three Essays on Military Strategy in Uganda* ( ) 10-11
62. Colin S. Gray, *Modern Strategy*, (Oxford, Oxford University Press, 1999),
63. Colin S. Gray, *Modern Strategy*, (Oxford, Oxford University Press, 1999),
64. Carl von Clausewitz, *On War*, (New York, Princeton University Press, 1993), 111

12

The Nexus between Historical Experience and Doctrine

'Military doctrine is what we believe about the best way to conduct military affairs.'

Drew and Don Snow

Not for the first time in military history, the Prussians are credited with a significant invention. This time its doctrine. The incomparable Prussians, began to revolutionize warfare through a number of innovations in the early 19th century. The principal innovation was the instituting of a General Staff (or what was called the 'Great German General Staff') as a result of the humiliating defeat Prussia suffered (courtesy of Napoleon) at Jena in 1806. The formation of a General Staff had been part of a package of reforms implemented by two precocious Prussian officers, Gerhard von Scharnhorst and August von Gneisenau. Carl von Clausewitz, was an associate of these reformers (although considerably younger than them) and an early instructor at the 'Kriegsakademie' (equivalent of a Staff College), another Prussian novelty. The General Staff was meant to be a body of elite military professionals, who incessantly made preparations for the next war.

The Prussian General Staff had an autonomy and influence on the state that was remarkable.

In 1857, Helmuth von Moltke (the elder) became Chief of the General Staff and set about refining this organization. He ensured that only the cream of the Prussian officer corps could join the General Staff. Every year, the Prussian Army's top 120 junior officers were identified by way of competitive exams to attend the Kriegsakademie. The curriculum at the academy was so rigorous that fewer than half of the class graduated. From these few graduands, von Moltke selected the best 12 for his personal mentoring as General Staff officers. Under von Moltke the chosen few undertook historical studies, attended annual maneuvers, participated in tactical exercises without troops (or 'TEWTS') and engaged in war games.

Von Moltke's intention was to create an elite system of senior staff officers and commanders that thought the same, what he referred to as the 'nervous system' of the Prussian army. In the great victories that the Prussian army was to achieve over the Danes, Austrians and French in the years to come, this 'nervous system' needed only to receive the briefest of instructions from von Moltke, in order to grasp his intent and execute.

Under von Moltke, the remit of the General Staff was extended into the infrastructure projects of the Prussian state. General Staff logistical calculations for the efficient movement of men and matériel in war were duly noted and implemented in the public works of Prussia. Prussia's railroads, bridges, roads and the telegraph system were all built with an eye to possible conflict with her neighbors. The General Staff became a machine whose sole purpose was the efficient and ruthless prosecution of decisive war.

The combination of these innovations was to have strategic effect beyond anyone's wildest imagination. The Prussian reforms would purchase the unification of Germany (with Prussia in prime position) by 'blood and iron'. Starting with the Schleswig-Holstein conflict with Denmark in 1864 then followed by the 'Seven Weeks War' with Austria in 1866 (that ended with the decisive battle of Königgrätz) and finally the Franco-Prussian war of 1870, the Prussian military reforms were resoundingly vindicated.

A developed railroad infrastructure ensured the rapid concentration of Prussia's armies on the borders of her adversaries. Both in the Seven Weeks War and the Franco-Prussian war, the efficient Prussians were able to utilize their more developed railroad networks to concentrate their armies a lot quicker than either the Austrians or the French. In 1866, the Prussians were able to utilize their five railway lines to mass 285,000 men on the Austrian border in less than 25 days, a feat the Austrians with only one railway line could not match. Then in the Franco-Prussian war, the Prussians concentrated 462,000 men on the French border; the French were only able to muster 270,000 soldiers. Von Moltke utilized telegraphs to communicate with his armies, but this mode of communication went only as far as the various army headquarters. Smaller formations had to make use of dispatchers on horse back to get messages through. All Prussian formations were drilled to 'march towards the sound of the guns', i.e. to converge wherever the fighting was raging. This assured that the Prussians would mass wherever the fighting was fiercest and, therefore, would maintain a local superiority in numbers.

In addition to Von Moltke's 'nervous system' (the German General Staff), the railroads and the telegraph system, technological improvements in German firearms generated unimaginable dividends. The accurate Prussian 'breech-loading needle gun' cut down swathes of Austrians at Königgrätz. The breech-loading needle gun could be operated while lying in the prone position or while advancing, whereas operators of the Austrian muzzle loading gun had to constantly stand up to re-load their rifles. This technological edge guaranteed that the Prussians massacred 44,000 Austrians at Königgrätz for only 9,000 Prussian dead. Again at the battle of Sedan in 1870 (August 30th -September 2nd) during the Franco-Prussian war, Von Moltke was to exploit these advantages to crush Emperor Napoleon III's Army of Chalon. The French lost 17,000 men with an additional 21,000 men captured for only 2,320 Prussian dead. The capture of Emperor Napoleon III (a nephew of Napoleon Bonaparte) in this battle was a humiliating blow for the French and assured the downfall of the Second French Empire. The battle of Sedan in 1870 was payback for the battle of Jena, sixty four years earlier.

Doctrine was an inevitable product of the German General Staff's obsession with efficiency in war. In 1870, a document entitled 'Regulations for the Instruction of the Troops in Field Service and the Exercises of Larger Units' was published; it was revised in 1887 and published again in 1908 as 'Field Service Regulations'. These 'regulations' were based on the German army's experiences in past wars. This historical experience was analyzed and pertinent lessons for the conduct of current and future operations were derived. Hence, military doctrine began as a compilation of tactics, techniques and procedures (TTPs) that were perceived to have worked in the past. Doctrine emerged as a result of historical experience when viewed through the prism of perceptive analysis. One may hasten to add that this is still how military doctrine is perceived today.

Doctrine, from the start was understood as comprising of methods a military organization believed were effective in a war situation, at a particular point in time. Two ideas are central to an understanding of doctrine. First of all doctrine represents what a military organization 'believes' to be efficacious in the conduct of operations. This implies that doctrine 'is the result of an examination and interpretation of the available evidence. In addition, it implies that the interpretation is subject to change should new evidence be introduced'[65]. This first concept is linked to the second vital idea, which is that doctrine is transient, it must of necessity change and evolve. Doctrine is not immutable; it is constantly changing driven by new conditions and realities.

One of the main drivers of doctrine (and its transient nature) is technology. Since technology is constantly evolving, what worked yesterday in the absence of present day technologies cannot be counted upon to be effective today. There is a popular military adage that goes, 'do not prepare to fight the last war', or words to that effect. There are numerous examples throughout military history where obsolete doctrine collided with a new form of warfare. Think of Saddam Hussein's much vaunted military machine (in 1990) and how it was pulverized by the U.S -led coalition fighting a new type of war. Saddam and his generals had expected to re-fight the Iran-Iraq war (where their forces had put forth a decent performance); however, they were quickly overwhelmed by superior U.S. technology. The Iraqis had not taken stock of the enormous advances in U.S. intelligence, surveillance, reconnaissance (ISR) assets, in precision guided munitions and in stealth technology. The Iraqi mechanized forces in their dug-outs in the Iraqi desert and in Kuwait were sitting ducks for U.S. precision guided bombs, fired from aircraft and ships. Saddam's doctrine was woefully inadequate for the war he was engaged in.

The historical nature of doctrine brings us to one of the fundamental motives for the writing of this book. As was described in the introduction, some of the people interviewed for this book were at pains to understand the relevance to the present day of past experiences. Some told me I should be focusing on present day operations. They did not immediately grasp the nexus between historical experience and current/future doctrine. Only in our history will we find the gems that will purchase future military successes. In the words of MacGregor Knox and Williamson Murray, 'The future is [very much] behind us'.

All successful militaries are built on the foundation of past experiences. U.S. doctrinal development in the twentieth century exhibited a strong inclination for technological solutions. AirLand Battle doctrine that emerged at the close of the 1973 Yom Kippur war, sought to harness the lethal precision of conventional munitions (anti-tank guided missiles had debuted in the Yom Kippur war and had been able to demonstrate great effectiveness against Israeli armor) against the anticipated hordes of Soviet armor that would sweep across western Europe if the 'Cold War' ever went hot. General William E. DePuy, an intelligent but rigid American officer was the father of AirLand Battle. DePuy envisaged that these precision guided munitions (PGMs) would be delivered by air platforms and would target the much feared second echelon of the Soviet 'shock' armies. This interdiction of Soviet reserves by 'smart' munitions, launched from aircrafts and artillery would allow 'windows of time' in which the numerically inferior U.S. and NATO forces could attrit Warsaw Pact forces at the frontlines. In 1991, NATO forces that had been prepared to fight an AirLand battle in the temperate plains of Germany were re-directed and used to crush Saddam's army in the deserts of Kuwait and southern Iraq.

This U.S. proclivity for technological solutions is firmly rooted in that nation's history. Knox and Murray are enlightening when they state: 'The obsessions of the technological utopians derive equally from the deeply and quaintly American belief that all human problems have engineering solutions...'[66]. American 'belief' in technology can be traced back to the Jeffersonian obsession with science and engineering. Thomas Jefferson (who rose to be the third president of the United States) passionately believed that the mastering and teaching of science was vital for the preservation of republican government (as opposed to royal tyranny) in the United States. Jefferson said, 'The value of science to a republican people, the security it gives to liberty by enlightening the minds of its citizens, the protection it affords against foreign power, the virtue it inculcates, the just emulation of the distinction it confers on nations foremost in it; in short, its identification with power, morals, order and happiness (which merits to it premiums of encouragement rather than repressive taxes), are considerations [that should] always [be] present and [bear] with their just weight'[67]. Consequently, from its founding in 1802, the United States Military Academy (Westpoint) offered a curriculum that emphasized engineering subjects. In fact, many of America's foremost engineers in the nineteenth century were educated at Westpoint. Those engineers built that nation's earliest roads, bridges, railways and harbors. Talk about having a productive army.

The case for a maneuverist approach to operations reverberates throughout this monograph. Maneuver was a central element of the resistance war. All the key battlefield successes (Masindi, Kabamba III, Kembogo and Kampala) were obtained through the application of maneuver. Even at Masaka and Mbarara, ostensibly straightforward examples of siege warfare (normally associated with attrition), maneuver was evident. The war in its entirety was an exercise in maneuver; this is in keeping with the practice of people's war, i.e. achieving a favourable 'correlation of forces'. A maneuverist approach to operations was the centerpiece of a brilliant guerrilla campaign conducted by the NRA in central and western Uganda. It is, therefore, an essential constituent of our military heritage.

What do we mean by a maneuverist approach to operations? A maneuverist approach is defined as, 'An approach to operations in which shattering the enemy's overall cohesion and will to fight is paramount. It calls for an attitude of mind in which doing the unexpected, using initiative and seeking originality is combined with a ruthless determination to succeed'[68]. This seems to have been the unwritten, unspoken creed of the NRA. It is in their actions that it is deduced that the defeat of the enemy by means other than the destruction of his mass is achieved through a maneuverist approach to operations.

Consider for a moment the stunning maneuverist victory the Israeli's achieved over an Egyptian force twice their size in the Sinai in 1967. With a force of 60,000 men organized into multi-brigade sized task forces (known as *ugdah's* in the IDF) and air superiority (achieved by surprise in the first hours of the conflict), the Israelis were able to rout a force of seven Egyptian divisions (five infantry and two armored). Central to the Israeli success was the adoption of a national defense strategy that exploited the maneuverist bias of leading Israeli commanders and the IDF as a whole. This strategy was based on a policy that sought to quickly carry any conflict with the Arabs away from Israeli cities and infrastructure, to fight the war on Arab soil. For this to happen, the Israelis had to rely on the instruments of maneuver: pre-emption; dislocation and disruption.

At 7.45 am (a time that had been determined as when the Egyptian air bases were most vulnerable to attack) on the 5th of June 1967, Israeli airstrikes caught the Egyptians completely offguard. The Israelis had 'pre-empted' the Egyptian build up, this surprise (as well as the strong break-in battles conducted by Israeli armor in the Sinai) were to seriously dent Egyptian morale. Many Egyptian commanders were unable to re-join their units until later that evening, on account of the Israeli superiority in the air. Field Marshal Amer, commander-in-chief of the Egyptian army and a close confidant of President Nasser, had been airborne (enroute to Sinai) when the airstrikes began. In the first few minutes of the war, Egyptian air defenses were restricted in their response to the Israeli sorties because of fear of shooting down the Field Marshal's aircraft (which was on its way back from Sinai). By the time he returned, Marshal Amer's airforce had been destroyed on the ground. These catastrophic events led to a plummeting of morale in the senior leadership of the Egyptian military, with

Amer contemplating suicide on a number of occasions. By 4.30 pm on the 6th of June, Amer's despair gave way to unconcealed panic; he ordered a general retreat of all Egyptian forces in the Sinai. The Israelis responded by pursuing the retreating Egyptians and attempting to block the exits to the Suez Canal. The Israelis had scored a massive victory that had been based on pre-emption, doing the unexpected, crushing the enemy's morale and aggression.

In conclusion, the advantages of a maneuverist approach to operations are clear. Fortunately, we have an illustrious history of maneuver warfare to build on. The independence and ability to innovate of our commanders is an advantage that we must encourage and nurture. Our commanders are already inclined to mission type orders (auftragstaktik) and improvisation. This is because of our background as a guerrilla army, with widely dispersed and largely autonomous sub-units. Our doctrine (which must be based on our historical experience) must espouse a maneuverist approach to war. Following from that the training, structuring and equipping of our forces must reflect the way we are wired (or programmed) to fight.

Notes

65. Military Doctrine by Denis Drew and Don Snow http://www.au.af.mil/au/awc/awcgate/readings/drew1.htm (accessed 18 January 2010)
66. Macgregor Knox, Williamson Murray, *The Dynamics of Military Revolution 1300-2050*, (New York, Cambridge University Press, 2001), 179
67. Thomas Jefferson on Politics and Government, http://etext.virginia.edu/jefferson/quotations/jeff1350.htm (accessed 23 April 2010)
68. Urban Operations in the Year 2020, http://ftp.rta.nato.int/public//PubFullText/RTO/TR/RTO-TR-071///TR-071-$$TOC.pdf (accessed 23 May 2010)

13

Epilogue: Maneuver in Our Future

> *'Yes, I think you're right, our war was based on maneuver'*
> Salim Saleh

Today in western militaries, maneuver warfare is automatically associated with the alleged 'revolution in military affairs' (RMA) that warfare seems to be embarking on. This new RMA is linked to the information revolution that the world is currently experiencing. Recent conflicts where U.S. led coalitions irreverantly swept aside opponents, have reinforced the notion that we are on the cusp of revolutionary changes in the conduct of warfare. This RMA, much like the RMAs that went before it, is linked to the great social, political and economic changes associated with the advent of a socio-economic revolution. In this case, we are talking about the information age. Just like the Prussians were able to utilize the railroads, telegraphic system, steamships and quick firing breech loading rifles that the industrial revolution availed, so to the U.S. and other advanced armies are working tirelessly to exploit the opportunities that the present explosion in information technology offers.

In line with this, these militaries propose to equip and field forces that will possess information dominance, i.e. 'networked' military units, utilizing computers and able to share (in real-time) precise information on the enemy. This information superiority will enable a common operating picture (COP) from tactical units up to the operational and strategic levels. This will facilitate rapid fire support for widely dispersed units (what is called the 'sensor to shooter loop') from any number of platforms. Networked forces can, therefore, field smaller, more mobile, but more lethal (in terms of firepower) units. The U.S. army for example is moving away from a reliance on divisions to an organization based on modular brigades.

This near omniscience on the battlefield (that the new RMA affords) will permit for the deployment of information age forces in a non-contiguous ('non-linear' battlefield). 'Non-contiguous' battlefield is a euphemism for the kind of counter-insurgency (asymmetric) wars western militaries anticipate they will be engaged in the 21st Century. Information age forces will be able to overwhelm the enemy by fighting the 'close' and 'deep' battles simultaneously. This will overwhelm the enemy's command and control systems and hopefully lead to a collapse of the enemy's defenses. Thereby achieving 'simultaneity' a key concept in the maneuverist approach to operations. 'Simultaneity' communicates the idea of overloading the enemy's command, control and communications systems (C3) by threatening to attack or by actually attacking multiple 'decisive points' simultaneously and throughout the area of operations (AO). It seeks to cause a collapse of the enemy's decision making system and hence facilitate a rapid and decisive victory.

'Precision strike' will permit networked forces to engage the enemy from a safe distance. This along with 'information operations' that use the electromagnetic spectrum to degrade the enemy's command, control, communications, computers, intelligence, surveillance and reconnaissance (C4ISR) systems, will essentially neutralize any enemy attempt to organize a coherent defense (related to the point in the preceding paragraph). Precision strike and information operations allow these networked forces to engage in what is called 'disengaged combat', i.e. being able to reach out and touch the enemy without him having any serious counter-attack capability.

The synergy of all these components of the new RMA will, it is believed, lead to the systemic collapse of most conventional opponents. The two wars against Iraq and the war to remove the Taliban from power in Afghanistan seem to vindicate this notion. Of course, even the vastly powerful U.S. military is re-learning a lesson (in Iraq and Afghanistan) that it seems to have forgotten after Vietnam, i.e. that an unconventional enemy utilizing a people's war strategy can present even the most powerful of armies with an intractable problem.

This contemporary association of maneuver warfare, with the anticipated RMA that certain hi-tech militaries are pondering, should not dissuade others (i.e. low tech militaries) from embracing the maneuverist faith. Maneuver warfare is as applicable today as it was in the time of Ntare V of Nkore. There is no shelf life on 'doing the unexpected, using initiative and seeking originality'. At the heart of the maneuverist approach are the three instruments: pre-emption; dislocation and disruption. None of these is particularly predicated on technological sophistication. The precepts of maneuver warfare can enhance doctrine that is based on exploiting a perceived technological superiority over an enemy, but they are not reliant on technology. Even low tech armies can exploit these principles of maneuver and should do so.

Fortunately in the Ugandan experience, we already have a solid maneuverist foundation to build on. For when the present day UPDF was still a guerrilla outfit, etching out an existence in the unforgiving bushes of Bulemezi, Ngoma and Singo, it survived through maneuver. In the hands of the gifted commanders of the NRA, all the instruments of maneuver were utilized to lay hold to a glorious and unexpected military victory. 'Physical dislocation' was the principal tool utilized by the NRA's premier force, the Mobile Brigade, as we saw in the battles of Masindi and Kabamba III. At Kembogo, Salim Saleh made use of a combination of maneuver and attrition to fight the most decisive battle of the entire resistance war. The UNLA's center of gravity was smashed at Kembogo and the war transitioned into the conventional or strategic counter-attack phase. At the battles of Masaka and Mbarara (barely three months after Kembogo) the NRA had not gathered sufficient strength to take the cities by direct attack. The NRA's commanders conjured up siege warfare and employed this technique to once again 'defeat the enemy without destroying his mass'. At the battle of Kampala, thanks to the Tanzanian arms secured by Yoweri Museveni, the NRA was able to overwhelm the capital city in two days of fighting. However, by the battle of Kampala, the enemy's will to fight had been crushed (chiefly by the battles of Kembogo and Katonga). The UNLA had become a shell of an army.

With this illustrious maneuverist heritage, the UPDF could promulgate a doctrine that underscores this legacy. Already ingrained in our field army is the practice of mission command or 'Auftragstaktik'. This practice, of telling people 'what to do and not how to do it' has its origins in our history as guerrillas, with widely dispersed semi-autonomous units. We should reinforce this practice in doctrine and training. Additionally, 'recon-pull' or placing the onus on good reconnaissance and then improvizing with the plan as we go should be a hallmark of our way of warfare.

Maneuver warfare, above all, emphasizes quality commanders, planners and soldiers. There has never been an army that won by maneuver that was not qualitatively better than its opposition. This is something we must strive to implement across the range of our training programs. We must actively seek and promote those individuals within our ranks who demonstrate a proclivity and knack for maneuver. Just as our history reveals there is no profit (or finesse) in seeking to destroy the entire physical strength of the enemy, overthrowing him by concentrating on the intangibles of war (or 'moral forces' in Clausewitz's words), i.e. his morale, his willpower and his fears is less bloody and more advantageous. If this holds true in the 21st century as it has for centuries, then maneuver warfare will continue to be in our collective futures!

Index

Acak Opon Smith (Brig.) 134
Adowa battle 5, 6
African nationalists 20
Akandwanaho Caleb (Gen.) 51, 78
Aksum 5
Ali, Chefe (Brig.) 52, 157, 176
Amin Idi (fr. Pres. Ug.) 18, 21, 44, 61, 194
Ankole Kingdom 4, 9, 63
Anti-Amin War 49, 66, 79, 93, 96
Asian Community (Ug.) 18

Banyankore 4, 10
Buganda 9, 11
Bukalabi disaster 82, 84, 86, 88, 90, 111, 129
Bukeni Patrick 23, 24
Bunyoro 9, 10, 11
Byaruhanga Akanga 70, 74, 80, 160, 171

Castro, Fidel 61, 71, 127
Chama Cha Mapinduzi (CCM) 53
Che Guevara 17, 43, 47, 127
Chemsford, Lord 8, 9
Chihandae, Julius 70, 157, 162
Chwezi Empire 9, 10

Clausewitz, Carl von 2, 26, 40, 46, 55, 85, 88, 106, 137, 191, 194, 198
Conventional warfare 91, 92, 138, 149, 196, 199

Democratic Republic of Congo (DRC) xii, 9, 114, 128, 190
Dingiswayo chief 6, 8

Frente de Libertacao de Mozambique (FRELIMO) 19, 39, 52, 53, 78
Front for National Salvation (FRONASA) 45, 50, 58, 61, 63, 64, 74, 79, 93

Great Lakes Region 76
Guerrilla warfare xvi, 91, 102, 112, 150

Incarceration of. *See* Akandwanaho Caleb (Gen.)

Kabamba garrison 115, 118, 122, 123
 first battle of 64, 65, 71, 72, 76
 third battle of 115, 122, 123, 127, 157
 Training School of 64, 67, 102
Kabundami II 10

Kafu River 97, 101, 104, 108
Kagame Paul (Pres. RW) 67, 76
Kagera Salient (TZ) 45, 92
Kagezi (major) 116, 117, 121
Kakonge John 19
Kanyankore, Tadeo 64, 69
Kashaka Stephen 96, 97, 99, 101, 112, 115, 129
Katonga battles 150
Katonga River 114, 147, 150, 162
Kaweweta military Cantonment 158
Kazimoto 22, 27, 28, 29, 30, 35
Kazini James (MG) 131, 132, 135, 137, 138, 144, 146, 185
Kembogo battle 137, 138, 149, 155, 172, 218
Kerim Peter 95, 98, 152, 158, 162
Kigongo Moses 127
Kikosi Maluum 45, 61, 63, 74, 79, 93
King's African Rifles (KAR) 50, 62
Koreta Ivan (Gen.) 52, 58, 152, 158, 162, 169
Kutesa Dora 81
Kutesa Pecos (MG) 81, 82, 96, 98, 99, 101, 129, 148
Kyaligonza, Matayo 162

Leonhard Robert xix, 2, 3, 7, 90, 137
Lord's Resistance Army (LRA) xii, 85
Lumumba Patrick 93, 96, 112, 115, 120, 129, 132, 146, 160, 176, 185
Lutaya Andrew 65
Luwero Triangle xiii, 82, 88, 90, 103, 127, 158, 173, 199

Machel Samora 52, 58
Magara Sam 66, 67, 74
Maluku estate episode xvi, 17, 18, 57, 73
Mande Samson 152, 158
Maneuver Warfare 15, 53, 123, 138, 202, 213, 215, 217, 219
Masindi Artillery 92, 97, 98
Mayanja River 104, 110, 113, 128, 130
Menelik II emperor 5, 6
Mobile brigade 81, 91, 95, 97, 98, 100, 102, 104, 107, 108, 112, 115, 118, 120, 125, 129, 130, 132, 135, 138, 139, 142, 157, 196
Mobuto Sese Seko 20
Moi Arap Daniel 159
Monduli Military Academy 74

Mugabi Hannington 66, 68, 69
Mugume Joram xviii, 81, 112
Muhangi Stanley 90, 93, 162
Mukwana Maumbe xix, 18, 21, 23
Museveni Yoweri Kaguta (Pres. Ug.) xiii, 4, 14, 22, 45, 48, 51, 52, 72, 78, 79, 110, 159, 165, 168, 188, 194
 as chairman of the high command 81, 90, 112
Mutambuka 11, 12
Mwebaze Jet 160
Mwesiga Martin 22, 24, 27, 30

Nabudere Wadada Sam 18
Nairobi Peace Accord 159, 162
National Resistance Army 3, 49, 53, 81, 82, 84, 93, 96, 100, 102, 110, 199
 high command of 90, 112
 warfare of 4
National Resistance Movement (NRM) 141
Ntare V 12, 14, 217
Nyerere Julius 19, 45, 52, 58, 151

Obote Milton (fr. Pres. Ug.) 18, 20, 23, 61, 94, 98, 110, 113, 128, 134, 139

Occidental military culture 4
Ochora Walter (Col.) 134
Ogole John LTC 118, 125, 128
Ojok, Oyite David 60, 61, 63, 74, 79, 80, 128, 134, 185
Okello Lutwa (Lt. Gen) 134, 141
Oketa James 143, 145
Okoya (Brigadier) 21
Ondoga ori Amaza 117, 119, 179

Parker Geoffrey 1
Peace negotiations (Ug.) 142
Political Indoctrination 50
Positional dislocation warfare 3, 120, 123
Proletarian revolution 50, 51
Protracted People's War 166, 173, 195

Revolutionary Warfare 33, 53
Royal Military Academy Sundhurst vii, 111
Rwaheru Valerian 24, 29, 33
Rwenzori Mountains 125
Rwigema Fred (MG) 51, 62, 78, 80, 81, 84, 88, 94, 95, 149, 157, 186

Safari 50 112, 126
Salim Saleh (Gen) xviii, 51, 52, 74, 78, 80, 81, 88, 90, 93, 96, 103, 112, 118, 128, 129, 143, 156, 165, 176, 180, 215, 218
Shaka Zulu 1, 6, 7, 15, 56
Sharon Ariel 106, 107
Siege warfare 153, 156, 211, 218

Tanzania Peoples Defence Forces (TPDF) 45, 198
Tewodros II emperor 5
Tinyefuza David 161, 176
Tshombe Moise 20
Tumwine Elly (Gen.) 49, 52, 53, 64, 66, 67, 69
Tzu, sun 2, 137, 191

Uganda National Liberation Army (UNLA) xiv, 3, 61, 63, 74, 76, 79, 93, 104, 108
Uganda National Rescue Front (UNRF) 82
Uganda Peoples' Congress (UPC) 19, 64, 167
Uganda Peoples' Defence Forces (UPDF) 84, 93, 95, 97, 103, 116, 134, 143, 169
Uganda Revolutionary Movement 50

West Nile Region 79, 82, 148
Zedong Mao xix, 44, 49, 104, 178, 196, 198
Zulu Empire 4, 14